VIZ GRAPHIC NOVEL

MAISON IKKOKU FAMILY AFFAIRS™

STORY AND ART BY

RUMIKO TAKAHASHI

CONTENTS

This volume contains
MAISON IKKOKU Part Two, #1 through #6 in their entirety

STORY & ART BY RUMIKO TAKAHASHI

English Adaptation/ Gerard Jones
Translators/ Matt Thorn & Toshifumi Yoshida
Touch-Up Art & Lettering/ Wayne Truman
Cover Design/ Viz Graphics
Editor/ Trish Ledoux
Assistant Editors/ Annette Roman & Toshifumi Yoshida
Managing Editor/ Satoru Fujii
Executive Editor/ Seiji Horibuchi
Publisher/ Keizo Inoue

First Published by Shogakukan, Inc. in Japan
Executive Editor/ Katsuya Shirai

Printed in Canada

Published by Viz Communications, Inc.
P.O. Box 77010 • San Francisco, CA 94107

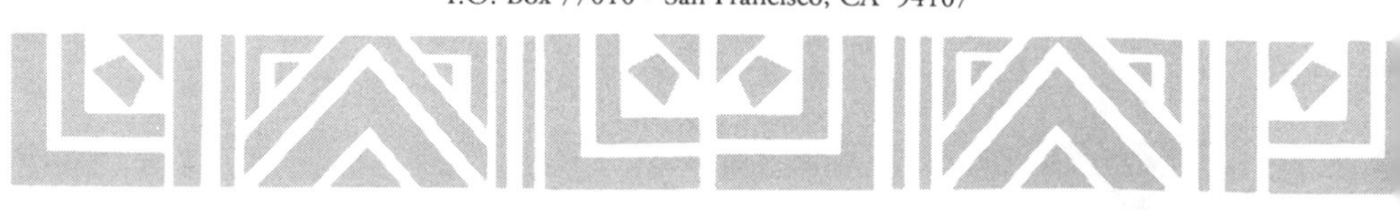

Part One

Intensive Care

OH, COACH MITAKA! WHAT A HIT!
FWOK
GET IT, KYOKO! GET IT!

OH!
KRRX!

WHUMP
KYOKO!
KYOKO, ARE YOU ALL RIGHT?
I'M FINE! I'M...

IT'S SPRAINED.
I SHOULDN'T HAVE HIT THE BALL SO HARD.
NO, PLEASE, IT ISN'T YOUR FAULT. I SHOULD HAVE...

I SHALL CARRY YOU TO THE HOSPITAL!
OH!
BUT... UM...
PLEASE SET ME DOWN. THERE'S REALLY NO NEED TO...
GLINT
ENJOY
NO.
OOOOO!
THUD
DON'T YOU THINK YOU'RE PUSHING IT?
WHO? ME?!
PLEASE DON'T MISJUDGE ME!
THIS IS MY DUTY AS A COACH!
OH?
SO IF I GET HURT YOU'LL CARRY ME THAT WAY?
UH-HUH. JUST WHAT I FIGURED.
BRRR.R

I REALLY AM SORRY.
I HATE TROUBLING YOU LIKE THIS.
FEH. WE ALL GOTTA HELP EACH OTHER SOMETIMES.

MAKE SURE YOU STAY *OUTSIDE* THE BED!
HA HA HA! YOU SHOULDN'T MAKE SUCH JESTS IN FRONT OF YOUR CHILD!
YES! PLEASE!

HI, KYOKO. I HEARD YOU GOT HURT.
ONLY A LITTLE.

ANYWAY, MACHO-MAN IS HERE TO SAVE THE DAY!
SINCE I CAUSED THIS TRAGEDY...
...I SHALL PERSONALLY SEE TO YOUR CARE UNTIL YOU ARE WELL!
BUT... BUT...

ANYWAY, I... I HAVE TO STAY IN BED FOR TWO DAYS, AT LEAST.
I HOPE I DON'T INCONVENIENCE YOU TOO MUCH AS TENANTS.
C'MON, DON'T WORRY ABOUT IT!

HEY! THAT'S MITAKA'S CAR!
WHAT'S *HE* DOING HERE SO LATE?
MAISON IKKOKU

CLAP CLAP
WHOOPWHOOP
WA-HA-HA-HA-HA!
WHAT IS THIS ?!
KYOKO-- ?
NOK NOK
COME IN!

WHAT ?!
WELCOME HOME !

KYOKO, WHAT'S WRONG?! ARE YOU SICK?!
WHADDA YOU CARE, COMIN' HOME SO LATE?!
YUSAKU, YOU NEED A DRINK !
WILL YOU TELL ME WHAT'S GOING ON?
WHAT KIND OF MAN ARE YOU? OUT RUNNING AROUND WHILE KYOKO'S SUFFERING!
WILL SOMEBODY TELL ME SOMETHING?!

IT'S GETTING LATE.
I SHOULD BE LETTING YOU REST.
THANK YOU FOR EVERYTHING.
OKAY! GET-WELL PARTY'S MOVING TO MY ROOM!
EVERYBODY UP! UP!
WHY DON'T YOU STAY OVER?
I... DON'T THINK SO.

KYOKO! I...I...
WHAT ARE YOU DOING, FOOL?!
KYOKO NEEDS HER SLEEP.
ZZZZZ

CHIRP CHIRP
TAP TAP
KYOKO? ARE YOU AWAKE YET?
COME ON IN, YUSAKU.
UM... IF THERE'S ANYTHING I CAN DO FOR YOU... ANYTHING AT ALL...
THANKS, BUT I'LL BE FINE.

DON'T YOU HAVE CLASSES THIS MORNING?
YOU SHOULD GET GOING.
I'LL SKIP TODAY'S CLASSES! YOU NEED ME!

YOU CAN'T AFFORD TO SKIP ANY CLASSES.
BUT... BUT...
WHAT ARE YOU DOING?!
BOTHERING A WOMAN IN HER BED! DISGUSTING!

SORRY FOR THE TROUBLE, MRS. ICHINOSE.
I'LL TAKE CARE OF THE MANAGER! YOU GO TO SCHOOL! GO!
ALL RIGHT ALREADY!

AND BEFORE YOU KNOW IT, IT'S AFTERNOON...
HELLO!

MITAKA? WHAT... WHAT...?
I'M GOING TO BORROW YOUR KITCHEN.
YOU NEED TO EAT SOME HEALTHY FOODS.
PLEASE, YOU REALLY DON'T HAVE TO...
THIS WAS MY FAULT!
IF...IF YOU INSIST.
HERE YOU ARE.
UM... THANK YOU...
PLEASE, DON'T THANK ME!
GOOD, ISN'T IT?
OH!
IT IS GOOD!
IT'S VERY GOOD!
YOU'RE A GREAT COOK!
IT'S A PASSION WITH ME.

IT WAS TOO GOOD. I ATE TOO MUCH.
OHHH...
'SCUSE US, KYOKO.
WE BROUGHT YOU SOME FOOD.
IT ISN'T MUCH, BUT PLEASE ACCEPT IT.
BUT...
OH, DEAR. I SUPPOSE I HAVE TO.
HOW IS IT?
DO YOU LIKE IT?
OH... YES. YES!
OHHH...
I'LL NEVER EAT AGAIN.
KYOKO?
TAP TAP
Y-YES, YUSAKU?

BOING

URK

I...I THOUGHT YOU MIGHT BE HUNGRY.
IT'S NOT MUCH, BUT... UH...
.....

HE LOOKS SO PATHETIC. HOW CAN I SAY NO?

TH-THANK YOU!

DO YOU LIKE IT?

OH...OF COURSE...
SHLURP

WHAT?! YOU GAVE HER BEAN CAKE AND OCTOPUS?
AND YOU GAVE HER RAMEN?!
I SHOULD GET UP.
I CAN'T HAVE THEM ALL TREATING ME LIKE AN INVALID.
SHE SHOULD'VE SAID NO!
SHE ATE ALL HER RAMEN-- AND SMILED AT ME!
SHE'S TOO GOOD FOR HER OWN GOOD!
THIS IS NO GOOD!
SHE COULD HAVE SERIOUS INDIGESTION!
WHOOMF
I'VE GOT IT!
MY ANTACID!

KYOKO !!
VMMM
MGR.
WHAT ?!

I'M COMING, KYOKO !
WAIT !

I'M NOT...
ANTACID

SCREECH!

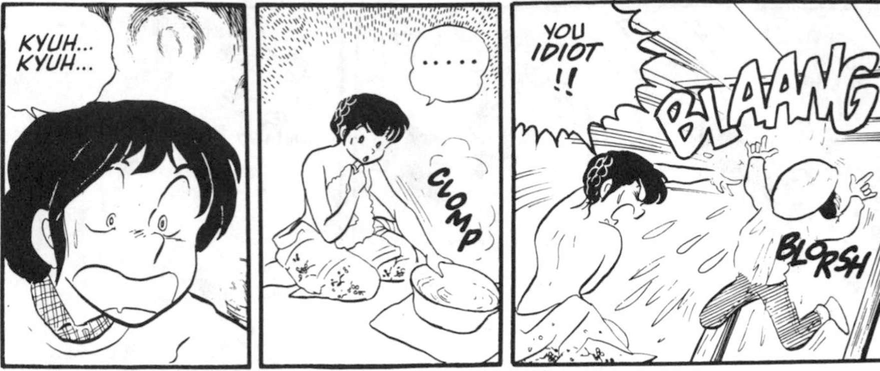
KYUH... KYUH...
......
CLOMP
YOU IDIOT !!
BLAANG
BLORSH
WHAT'S HAPPENING ?!
TMTMTMTM
SLAM
OH... NOTHING !
KYOKO! ARE YOU ALL RIGHT ?!
BAM
I'M FINE !!
BAM
YAAAA!!
SO! JUST WHEN SHE CAN'T RUN AWAY FROM YOU, YOU STRIKE!
DON'T LOOK !
WHAT IN THE...
SQUEEE
HEY! WAIT A MINUTE !

YOU ANIMAL !!
WHAP
LISTEN TO ME !
YOU WON'T TALK YOUR WAY OUT OF THIS ONE, ANIMAL!
YOU GOT IT WRONG !
PLEASE...

KYOKO, I'M SORRY I BARGED IN ON YOU!
PEEK
ALL RIGHT! NOW JUST GET OUT!
I'M SORRY !!
SLAM
GRRRR

ANTACID ?

WAS THAT IT...?
SKWIK WIK

.....
GLMP

YOU OVERATE ?
YES. MY STOMACH'S A LITTLE UPSET.
IT'S SO EMBARRASSING.
THAT'S TOO BAD. I WAS LOOKING FORWARD TO THIS.
UM... KYOKO? CAN I... COME IN?
TAP TAP
ALL RIGHT.
I'M SORRY ABOUT...
GASP
YOU !
KRRACKLE
WELL. HELLO.
WHAT HAPPENED TO YOUR FOREHEAD ?
I... UH... I...
IS THAT WHERE I HIT YOU WITH THE PAIL?
FORGET IT, FORGET IT, IT WAS MY FAULT.

I SHOULDN'T HAVE THROWN IT SO HARD.
I CAN'T BLAME YOU.
WELL, I DON'T WANT TO WASTE THIS--SO I'LL COOK IT.
I...I REALLY DON'T...
WHY DON'T YOU EAT IT, YUSAKU ?
HUH ?!
MITAKA IS A WONDERFUL COOK!
HMPH !
HE JUST WANTS AN EXCUSE TO KEEP HANGING AROUND.
SIZZLE
PLEASE! EAT!
YEAH. THANKS.
BET IT TASTES LIKE CR--

BUT NEITHER ONE SEEMED TO HEAR HER...

PIYO

Part Two

Shadows on the Heart

SSSHHHHH

SPLASH SPLASH

OH, DEAR, OH, DEAR...

PATTA PATTA PATTA PATTA
BLOOP BLOOP

UM... HERE.
HM ?
KOZUE... ?
YOU REMEMBER !

THANK YOU FOR THIS.
DON'T MENTION IT. I WASN'T DOING ANYTHING ELSE.
THINK OF SOMETHING TO TALK ABOUT...
IS YUSAKU AT SCHOOL ?
Y-YES !

HE SHOULD BE HOME BY DUSK.
DOES HE ALWAYS GO HOME SO EARLY ?
ONLY ON MONDAYS AND WEDNESDAYS. HE GETS HOME AROUND EIGHT ON TUESDAYS AND FRIDAYS, AND TEN ON THURSDAYS BECAUSE OF HIS TUTORING JOB.
OH.

YOU SEEM TO KNOW HIS SCHEDULE AWFULLY WELL.
WELL, I'M...

...I'M HIS APARTMENT HOUSE MANAGER!
MM.
SO THAT'S THE REASON?

OF COURSE IT IS!
THEN YOU KNOW ALL THE OTHER TENANTS' SCHEDULES TOO.
A-CHOO

WOW! THAT'S PRETTY GOOD!
OH, OF COURSE!
JUST DON'T ASK ME TO PROVE IT!

OH!
MR. SOICHIRO! WHAT ARE YOU DOING?!

I...I DON'T MIND. REALLY.
YOUR SKIRT! I'M SO SORRY!
A-CHOO

CAN YOU COME IN? I WANT TO GET THAT OUT BEFORE IT STAINS.
THAT WOULD BE GREAT.

SSSHHHH
I FEEL TERRIBLE ABOUT THIS. GO AHEAD AND WEAR MY SKIRT UNTIL IT DRIES.
YEESH! THE WAIST IS TIGHT.
POIK
I'LL MAKE US SOME TEA.
IF YOU INSIST.
THINK OF SOMETHING TO TALK ABOUT.
SAY. WHAT DO YOU THINK OF YUSAKU?
WHAT?!
WHAT DO I...I MEAN...
WHAT DO YOU MEAN BY THAT?
YOU'RE AROUND HIM A LOT, RIGHT?
WHAT KIND OF PERSON IS HE?
WELL...
...THAT'S HARD TO SAY...

ARE THERE ANY OTHER GIRLS HE GOES OUT WITH ?
NO, I... I'D SAY YOU'RE THE ONLY ONE.
REALLY ?!
YES.
HEE HEE
shff
SAY. YOUR BOYFRIEND'S PRETTY HANDSOME !
WHO ?!
HER BRAIN DOESN'T STAY IN ONE PLACE LONG.
THE MAN YOU WERE WITH WHEN I FIRST MET YOU.
OH, MITAKA! HE'S JUST A FRIEND.
NO !!
YES !
YOU DON'T HAVE A BOY-FRIEND?!
WELL, YOU SEE...

OH!
YOU'RE A...
...A WIDOW ?!
I'M SORRY! I NEVER KNOW WHEN TO KEEP MY MOUTH SHUT!
PLEASE, IT'S ALL RIGHT.
SSSHHHHH
BUT IT DOES MAKE ME REMEMBER...
KYOKO!

I SAW MR. OTONASHI IN THE LOBBY!
REALLY ?!
SAY--DOES HE HAVE AN UMBRELLA ?
GOOD IDEA... BUT HE'S GOT ONE!
WHAT ARE YOU DOING ?
GO ON WITHOUT ME!
BYE !
FORGET IT. WHEN THAT OTONASHI APPEARS, SHE'S BEYOND HOPE.
KYOKO-- !
.....

OH
!
DUMMY
!

BRRR!
COLD
!

TAP
TAP
TAP

WHY, MR.
OTONASHI
!
SSSHHHHH
HM
?

CARE
TO
JOIN
ME?
O-
OKAY.

YOU'RE
IN MY
THIRD
CLASS,
RIGHT?
MM-HM.
KYOKO
CHIGUSA.

MISS CHIGUSA ?
YES ?

ISN'T THIS CHILLY ?
VOOP
YOU'LL CATCH A COLD.

SSSHHHHH

THAT WAS A PRETTY WEIRD STUNT.

IT SEEMED LIKE A GOOD IDEA AT THE TIME.

......

HE WAS A TEACHER ?

JUST A GUEST LECTURER.

AND... MY FIRST LOVE.

YOU MARRIED YOUR FIRST LOVE ? THAT'S WONDERFUL.

.....

YUSAKU... HE...

YES ?

HE LOOKS A LOT LIKE MY FIRST LOVE.
OH!

OF COURSE IT WAS ONE OF THOSE ONE-WAY THINGS.

WHAT WAS HE LIKE?

HE WAS WONDERFUL!

EXCEPT...

...HE LOOKED LIKE YUSAKU!

SAY. YOU STILL LOVE YOUR HUSBAND, DON'T YOU?

HM?

OH. YES.

YUSAKU IS LATE, ISN'T HE?

YOU'RE RIGHT. HE'S USUALLY HOME BY NOW.

I'M HOME!

YUSAKU! WHERE WERE YOU ?!
HUH ?
FLAP FLAP
KOZUE WAS HERE UNTIL A LITTLE WHILE AGO.
WHAT ?!
SHE CAME HERE ?!
Y-YES.
YOU SHOULD CALL HER.
SHE WAITED QUITE A WHILE FOR YOU.
BUT... BUT WHY... I MEAN...
WHAT ARE ARE YOU TALKING ABOUT ?
SHE AND I... WE... YOU KNOW... I DON'T...
I DON'T NEED TO CALL HER!
WE AREN'T LIKE THAT !
YUSAKU, WAIT...
TAP TAP
REALLY !
HEY, KYOKO !
YES, MRS. ICHINOSE ?

C'MERE A SECOND.
WHAT IS IT?
THE FLUNKOUT'S GIRL-FRIEND WAS HERE?
YUSAKU IS NOT FLUNKING ANYMORE.
WHAT'D YOU TALK ABOUT? DID YOU FIGHT?
WHAT WOULD WE FIGHT ABOUT?
CREEP CREEP
BOOP BOOP
HI, KOZUE?
IT'S YUSAKU.
I HEARD YOU CAME BY.
WHAT'S UP?
OH, YEAH? THEN YOU WANT TO GET TOGETHER TOMORROW?
SCHOOL? I'LL SKIP IT.
SNEAKING AROUND, EH?
YOU HEAR THAT? YOU JEALOUS?
NOT ME.
HE'S SUCH A FOOL.
CREEP CREEP CREEP

THE NEXT DAY...
YUSAKU!
YEAH?
WOULD YOU RETURN KOZUE'S UMBRELLA?
DO WHAT?
IT HAD STOPPED RAINING WHEN SHE LEFT AND SHE FORGOT IT.
BUT I'M ON MY WAY TO SCHOOL!
OH? I THOUGHT YOU WERE SKIPPING SCHOOL TO SEE KOZUE!
GAK
HOW'D YOU KNOW ABOUT THAT?
BECAUSE I'M THE MANAGER.
BUT...BUT SHE AND I... WE AREN'T...
YOU SHOULDN'T SNEAK AROUND LIKE THIS.
HUH?
YOU'LL DISAPPOINT KOZUE.
YOU'RE GOING TO RUIN HER IMAGE OF HER FIRST LOVE.
HER WHAT?!

MAYBE I SHOULDN'T SAY IT...
SAY IT! SAY IT!
WHAT'S THIS ABOUT THE "IMAGE OF HER FIRST LOVE"?
WELL... UM...
IT SEEMS YOU LOOK JUST LIKE HER FIRST LOVE.
YEAH?
MEANING I'M NOT HER FIRST LOVE, HUH?
HE WAS SUPPOSED TO BE WONDERFUL.
SAY WHAT?
SHE SAID HE WAS WONDERFUL!
SO I THINK YOU SHOULD BE MORE HONEST. FOR KOZUE.
HMMM...
IT'S NOT LIKE KYOKO DOESN'T KNOW MY FEELINGS.
AT LEAST, SHE SHOULD KNOW!
WHAT'S GOING ON, ANYWAY?
A LITTLE WHILE AGO SHE WAS JEALOUS.

HI, YUSAKU!
HI.
BEEN WAITIN' LONG, KID?
SHE TOLD YOU ?!
YEAH.
I'M SORRY. ARE YOU MAD?
WHY SHOULD I BE?
YOU DON'T MIND BEING SEEN AS ANOTHER MAN'S IMAGE?
HA HA, OF COURSE NOT!
NOT TOO MUCH, ANYWAY.
BUT I WISH YOU COULD SEE ME AS ME.
OH, I DO!
SAY. DON'T YOU THINK KYOKO'S WONDERFUL?
TELEPHONE

SHE TOLD ME ABOUT HER HUSBAND YESTERDAY.
SHE DID ?!
IT'S SO ROMANTIC.
IF KYOKO TALKED ABOUT THAT...
SSSHHHHH
SHE MUST HAVE REALLY LOVED HIM.
IT MUST BE WONDERFUL TO MARRY SOMEONE YOU LOVE SO MUCH.
.....
BUT HE'S DEAD NOW...
YEAH...

YUSAKU, PLEASE DON'T DIE! OKAY?
HUH?

I DON'T WANT YOU TO DIE.

HA HA HA!
WHAT ARE YOU SAYING?

RRMMMBBLLL

SO. HE'S STILL THERE.
SOICHIRO OTONASHI.

KYOKO'S A FOOL!
TYING HERSELF TO A DEAD MAN LIKE THAT!
BLOP
BLOP

SSSHHHHH
WHAT'S WRONG WITH ME?!

YUSAKU ?
SSSHHHHH
CARE TO JOIN ME?
SSSHHHH
.....
NO THANKS. I WANT TO BE ALONE.
BUT YOU'LL CATCH A COLD!
I DON'T CARE !

PLISH PLISH

DAMN! SHE DOESN'T KNOW HOW I FEEL!

BUT SHE HAS TO!

AH-CHOOO

SSSHHHH

......

SORRY. IS THE OFFER STILL GOOD?

AHCHOO

SEE? I TOLD YOU YOU'D CATCH A COLD.

Part Three

Knit-Picking

RENT.
FOOD.
MISCELLANEOUS.
IF I SPEND MY PART-TIME WAGES ON GOING HOME...
...I HARDLY HAVE ANYTHING LEFT OVER.

TWO THOUSAND YEN AND CHANGE. WHOOPEE.

CAN'T BUY ANYTHING FANCY ON THAT!

SHOULD I JUST NOT GIVE HER A PRESENT?

NO, NO. CHRISTMAS IS THE ONLY TIME I CAN DO ANYTHING NICE FOR HER... OPENLY.

IT'S OKAY IF IT'S CHEAP, RIGHT?

IT'S THE THOUGHT THAT COUNTS! YEAH!

PLUS I NEVER GAVE HER THAT THING I BOUGHT HER LAST YEAR.

OKAY. SO TOMORROW I BUY KYOKO SOMETHING.

FWUMP

SHE HASN'T SHOWN HERSELF FOR DAYS!

BUT WHAT'S GOING ON WITH HER, ANYWAY?

YUUU-SAKU!
TELEPHONE!
YOW! COMING!
HUH?
HWOOOO
VROOOM
WOULD YOU KEEP IT DOWN?!
CLICK
AARGH!
TOOM
BLAST HER! SHE COULD AT LEAST HAVE LET ME SEE HER BACK!
HELLO?
OH! HI, KOZUE!
TOMORROW? SURE.
I HAVE TO GO SHOPPING ANYWAY, SO RIGHT AFTER THAT...
RIGHT. SEE YA.
SHOO!
AKEMI
CALL BAR

CAN'T I HAVE ANY PRIVACY, MRS. ICHINOSE?
JUST BECAUSE YOUR GIRLFRIEND CALLS DOESN'T MEAN YOU CAN STAMPEDE LIKE A HERD OF ELEPHANTS!
THE PHONE'S NOT GOING TO RUN AWAY!
I WASN'T WORRIED ABOUT THE PHONE!

MGR

IF YOU WANT TO TO SEE KYOKO, JUST KNOCK!
I HAVEN'T GOT ANY REASON TO.
MGR

SO MAKE UP A REASON!
YOU HAVE TO BE BOLDER! LIKE MITAKA!
I GUESS I'M JUST NOT THAT SLICK!

NEXT DAY...
LATER!

SEE YOU!
JUST HER VOICE AGAIN TODAY.

MARKET
CHRISTMAS BARGAINS ALL DAY EVERY DAY
WonderLand
DISCOUNT STORE
FOR ME?
YEP!
WELL, AT LEAST NOW I'LL HAVE A REASON TO KNOCK.
IT'S THE BARE-BONES LIFE FROM HERE ON!
TWO THOUSAND YEN EXACTLY.
WHAT LOVELY EARRINGS!
THANK YOU!
YOU MEAN... YOU'VE BEEN HOLED UP IN THERE THESE LAST FEW DAYS...
I PUT MY HEART AND SOUL INTO KNITTING THIS.
YOU DO?!
ACTUALLY, YUSAKU, I HAVE SOMETHING FOR YOU, TOO!

KNITTING FOR YOU, YUSAKU! JUST FOR YOU!
OH, KYOKO--
KLLONG

SALE
NNGH
Coffe

I'VE GOT TO CURE MYSELF...
...OF THIS DAYDREAMING!
merry Christ

YUSAKU!
TELEPHONE
HI.

WHAT HAPPENED?! YOU'RE BLEEDING!
HUH--?

WAIT. I'LL GET A HANKIE.
'SOKAY. I'LL USE MY OWN.

KLUNK

SO. YOU WANTED TO SEE ME...?
Special
YEAH! IT'S A DAY EARLY, BUT...

MERRY CHRISTMAS!
urk!
GIFT

TH-TH-THANK YOU! WHAT... WHAT...
I KNITTED IT MYSELF. IT'S NOT GREAT, BUT...
A HAT?
TRY IT ON!

THERE!
OH, IT'S CUTE!
OH, GREAT!
I DIDN'T EVEN THINK ABOUT KOZUE!
hee hee

BUT SINCE SHE GAVE ME SOMETHING...
...I GUESS I'VE GOTTA...
REST ROOM

MERRY CHRISTMAS.
BINK
OO!

OH, MY! EARRINGS!

THEY'RE SO SOPHISTICATED!
THEY'RE... THEY'RE PERFECT FOR YOU!

THANK YOU! I'M SO HAPPY!
HEH. ME TOO.

IDIOT! IDIOT! IDIOT!
GRR GRR GRR
THE ONLY THING THAT'LL CURE MY WAFFLING IS DEATH!
Welcome

HWOOOO
I'M SO HAPPY!
SO HAPPY!
SO HAPPY!
HAT'S WARM.
SHE REALLY IS SWEET.
SO EXCITED BY MY GIFT.
MAYBE IT'S BETTER THIS WAY...
I'M HOME!
WELCOME BACK!
JUST THE VOICE AGAIN.
GUESS I'LL JUST GIVE UP...
YUSAKU?

KYOKO ?!
NO KIDDING !
SORRY I'VE BEEN SUCH A STRANGER LATELY.
WHAT'VE YOU BEEN DOING IN THERE?!
OH, NO.
MERRY CHRISTMAS !
YOU MEAN... FOR ME ?!
I'VE BEEN KNITTING FOR DAYS !

NOW, IF YOU'LL FORGIVE ME, I NEED TO GET SOME REST!
I'VE BEEN STAYING UP THE LAST FEW NIGHTS.
OH, KYOKO!
YAWN
THANK YOU! THANK YOU!
SOB
OH, I'M SO HAPPY!
I...HAVE TO GET HER SOMETHING!
DOOOOOMMM
HEY NO, YUSAKU. WHY AREN'T YOU DRINKING?
ISN'T IT A LITTLE EARLY FOR SPRING CLEANING?
SHUT UP! I'M LOOKING FOR SOMETHING!
WE'RE HAVING A PARTY AT YOUR BAR TOMORROW!
CAN'T YOU HOLD OFF DRINKING UNTIL THEN?
I'M A WAITRESS. I CAN'T DRINK AT WORK.
YOU NEVER LET THAT STOP YOU.

THAT'S WEIRD.
I THOUGHT I STUCK IT IN HERE.

AHA!

WHAT IS IT?
......
OH, HEH HEH. JUST THAT I.D. I THOUGHT I'D LOST.
I SEE.
LEMME SEE IT!

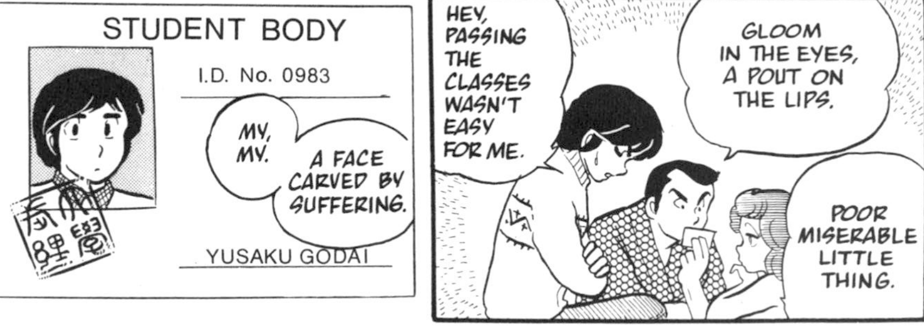
STUDENT BODY
I.D. No. 0983
YUSAKU GODAI
MY, MY.
A FACE CARVED BY SUFFERING.
HEY, PASSING THE CLASSES WASN'T EASY FOR ME.
GLOOM IN THE EYES, A POUT ON THE LIPS.
POOR MISERABLE LITTLE THING.

I WAS ONLY MIS-ERABLE BECAUSE YOU GUYS KEPT PICKING ON ME!
WE STILL PICK ON YOU.
WE SEE NO REASON TO STOP.
EVERY BOARDING HOUSE NEEDS A CLOWN.
WAIT A MINUTE--!

ANYWAY, CONGRATULATIONS ON FINDING YOUR I.D.
NOW LET'S DRINK.
PRRRR
HOLD IT!
I WASN'T LOOKING FOR MY I.D.!
GOOD NIGHT!
AKEMI, SLEEP IN YOUR OWN ROOM!
TOO MUCH TROUBLE.
I'LL TAKE ADVANTAGE OF YOU!
JUST TRY IT.
I'M SO GLAD YOU FEEL SAFE!
ZZZZZZZZ
NOT HERE.
NOT HERE.
NOT HERE.
HEY!
A HUNDRED YEN!
AND WHAT CAN I GET WITH THAT? A SODA?

YAAA!
WHAP

SHNOR SHNOR
SHNOR

AARGH! DON'T SLEEP LIKE THAT!
FWOMP
SHNOR
SHNOR

WHAT...?
WHAT...?

YES!

YES!

YES!

I HAVE FOUND IT !!
TA-DUMM
THE PRESENT I NEVER GAVE!
TWINK
TWINK
TWINK
SORRY IT'S NOT WRAPPED.
WHAT A CUTE BROOCH.
THANKS VERY MUCH.
FOR ME?
UM... ARE YOUR EYES RED?
I WAS... UH... READING LATE.
GUESS I'LL TAKE A NAP.

SUDDENLY IT'S EVENING...
YUSAKU? IT'S TIME FOR THE PARTY!
THIS SCARF'S SO WARM!
I'M GLAD. IT LOOKS GOOD ON YOU.
IT MATCHES YOUR HAT!
OH. HEH HEH. AND THAT BROOCH LOOKS GOOD ON YOU.
DOES IT REALLY?
I WAS WONDERING IF I COULD STILL WEAR SOMETHING AS YOUNG AS THIS.
WHAT ARE YOU SAYING? YOU'RE STILL YOUNG!
YOU'RE RIGHT. I'M STILL ONLY 22.
22...
TWO YEARS OLDER. ONLY TWO...
THAT'S NO OBSTACLE TO MARRIAGE.
JUST TWO YEARS...

OH, THERE'S SHUN!
WELL, HELLO.
YOU GOING TO THE PARTY TOO, MITAKA?
LET'S GO TOGETHER!
YOU MUST BE SENSITIVE TO THE COLD, YUSAKU.
FOR SOMEONE YOUR AGE.
YOU SAID IT!
I'M LUCKY THAT THIS SCARF IS REALLY WARM!
AFTER ALL, KYOKO PUT HER HEART AND SOUL INTO IT.
REALLY? KYOKO KNITTED THAT HERSELF?
HOW 'BOUT *THAT*, PAL?
SPEECHLESS, HUH?
WELL, WHAT DO YOU KNOW?

IT *IS* GETTING A LITTLE CHILLY, ISN'T IT?
WHIP
I'LL PUT MINE ON, TOO!
KYOKO REALLY *DOES* KNIT A WARM SCARF!
YOU KNOW, YOU'RE RIGHT!
OH! THANKS!
YOUR USE OF DIFFERENT COLORS WAS VERY CLEVER!
BUT I GUESS IT WASN'T SO IMAGINATIVE OF ME TO MAKE THE SAME SCARF!
DON'T BE SILLY!

YOU THINK YOU'RE SPECIAL? GUESS AGAIN!
DOES THIS MEAN SHE FEELS THE SAME ABOUT HIM AS ABOUT ME?
WHAT IS IT ABOUT ME SHE DOESN'T LIKE?
WHAT'S SHE MEAN BY GIVING US THE SAME THING?
NOT TRYING TO HAVE IT BOTH WAYS, IS SHE?
CHACHAMARU
HI, MRS. MANAGER!
HI, KENTARO!
BAR
GH
I'M GLAD.
THANKS FOR THE SCARF! IT'S REALLY WARM!

AK!

THANK YOU, KYOKO!
I'LL TREASURE IT FOREVER!
IT'S JUST SO WARM!

YOU ALL TOOK SUCH GOOD CARE OF ME WHEN I SPRAINED MY ANKLE...
...THIS IS JUST MY WAY OF SAYING "THANK YOU" AND "MERRY CHRISTMAS" AT THE SAME TIME.
AHA!

WE ALL MATCH!
SO WE DO.
YEAH. SWELL.
I DIDN'T HAVE TIME TO COME UP WITH DIFFERENT PATTERNS.
YOUR USE OF DIFFERENT COLORS WAS VERY CLEVER!
WA HA HA HA HA HA!
HEY, SWEETIE, MAKE ONE FOR THIS OLD MAN, TOO!

Part Four

Ring in the Nude

TOKYO...
DECEMBER 30...
YOU'RE NOT GOING HOME FOR NEW YEAR'S, YUSAKU?
I'M GOING HOME ON NEW YEAR'S DAY, IN THE EVENING.

THINK OF TRADITION! END THE YEAR WITH YOUR FAMILY!
CAN'T HELP IT. I'M WORKING THE 31ST TO EARN THE MONEY TO GET HOME.
DIDN'T YOUR FAMILY SEND YOU TRAIN MONEY?
I SPENT IT ALL.
NO ROOM FOR SYMPATHY, HM?

WHAT ARE YOU GOING TO DO, MR. YOTSUYA?
GOING HOME, AS I SHOULD.
I WAS ABLE TO GET SOME TIME OFF.

LOOKS LIKE YOU HAVE TIME OFF ALL YEAR LONG.
WHAT KIND OF WORK DO YOU DO?
THAT'S MY BUSINESS.
BUT YOU, YUSAKU! HOW PATHETIC TO GREET THE NEW YEAR ALONE IN THIS DINGY ROOM.
AW, LEMME ALONE.

YOU DON'T EVEN HAVE A TV!
THE COLD WILL BE PIERCING!
THERE'S NOTHING COLDER THAN A HOLIDAY...SPENT ALONE!
NOTHING SADDER.
DOOM
OH, YOU'LL BE SO LO-O-O-ONELY!
IT RENDS MY HEART.
WAIT! YOU'RE NOT GOING HOME EITHER!
WHAT ARE YOU MAKING ME FEEL SO BAD FOR?
WHO, ME?
I'M GONNA WATCH NEW YEAR'S EVE TV IN KYOKO'S ROOM!
WHAT? WITH KYOKO?!
OH-HO!
KYOKO ISN'T GOING HOME?
I DON'T GET IT. BUT SHE SAYS SHE'LL BE HERE.
SHOOP
IN KYOKO'S ROOM...
AREN'T YOU JEALOUS?

MAN, I'M GONNA BE LONELY.
LISTEN TO THIS WHINER!
DO YOU WANT TO COME TOO?
YOU MEAN... CAN I? CAN I?
THE MORE THE MERRIER!
THAT'S TRUE, THAT'S TRUE!
COMES THE DAWN...
YUSAKU'S COMING, TOO?
PIYO PIYO
THAT'S OKAY, ISN'T IT?
IT'S FINE. THE MORE THE MERRIER.
I'M OFF TO WORK!
WORK HARD!
UH...I'LL COME BY ABOUT NINE WITH SOME SOBA NOODLES.
I'M WORKING AT A NOODLE JOINT.
HA HA! EARNING YOUR NEW YEAR'S SOBA!
THAT MAKES THINGS SIMPLER!

YUSAKU, LET'S WALK TOGETHER.
HAVE A GOOD NEW YEAR'S.
YOU TOO. SAFE TRIP!
WONDER WHERE "HOME" IS FOR HIM.
HMM...

AS ON PAST NEW YEAR'S EVES, SHOPPERS THRONG TO THIS MALL...
KYOKO!
COMING!
NOK NOK

WE'RE OFF FOR THE HOLIDAY!
YOU'LL BE BACK ON THE FOURTH, RIGHT?
HURRY UP, DAD!
OH, DON'T BOTHER SEEING US OFF!
HAPPY NEW YEAR!
AT LAST...
SLAM
...THE CLEANING AND COOKING ARE DONE!

AND ANOTHER YEAR COMES TO A CLOSE, SOICHIRO.
PLEASE KEEP WATCHING OVER ME.
RRING
MAISON IKKOKU.
JUST A MOMENT, PLEASE.
HI, THIS IS AKEMI.
WHAT'S THAT?
SKIING ?! REALLY ?!
SOMEBODY CANCELED. THERE'S A TRAIN TICKET IF YOU WANT IT.
OF COURSE I WANT IT!
THEN MEET US AT UENO STATION AT SIX!
PANT PANT PANT
A CHANCE TO SKI?
UM... YEAH...
BUT I GUESS IT WOULDN'T BE SO GOOD...
...LEAVING YOU WITH YUSAKU.
OH!
OH.
UH-OH.

I'LL TELL THEM I CAN'T GO.
WHAT ?!
SIGH
AKEMI...
YOU WANT TO GO SKIING, DON'T YOU?
WELL... YEAH, BUT...
...IT WOULDN'T BE...
THEN GO.
BUT...
BUT YUSAKU, HE'S A...
OH, PLEASE! YOU THINK TOO MUCH, AKEMI!
ARE YOU SURE YOU'LL BE OKAY?
YOU HAVE TO TRUST YUSAKU MORE!
YOU'RE RIGHT.
OF COURSE I AM.
BINK
BINK
WELL, THEN...I'D BETTER GET READY!
PANT PANT
SOICHIRO...
PLEASE WATCH OVER ME!

PUBLIC BATHS
LAUNDRY
WHAT SHOULD I DO?
WELL, I'VE GOT EVERY-THING I COULD...
...TO KEEP THE MOOD FROM GETTING DANGER-OUS.
KYOKO!
OH!
ISN'T AKEMI WITH YOU?
N-N-NO, SHE... SHE...
SHOULD I TELL HIM SHE WON'T BE HERE?
SNIFF
MMM.
YOUR HAIR SMELLS GREAT.
I...UH... I JUST WASHED IT!
WELL, I'LL SEE YOU LATER!
O-OKAY!

I'M SURE I'M WORRYING ABOUT NOTHING.
BOUTIQUE
GOD, BUT THE SMELL OF FRESH-WASHED HAIR TURNS ME ON!
CLOSED JAN. 1-3

THIS WOULD BE SO GREAT IF AKEMI WASN'T THERE.

DID YOU EVER DREAM WE WOULD SPEND NEW YEAR'S EVE ALONE TOGETHER, KYOKO?
IT HAD TO HAPPEN, YUSAKU! WHY DO YOU THINK I WASHED MY HAIR?

MY DARLING... MAY I ?
OH, YES !

KLONG
KRAAAK

COME ON IN!
HAPPY TO!
THREE ORDERS OF NEW YEAR'S SOBA!
WHY, THANK YOU!
WHERE'S AKEMI?
UM...WOULD YOU LIKE COFFEE OR TEA?
COFFEE, PLEASE.
WHERE'S AKEMI?
DO YOU TAKE SUGAR?
UH-HUH.
FINE.
RRRRING
HELLO?
HI, KYOKO! IT'S AKEMI!
I JUST GOT TO THE HOTEL.
IS YUSAKU THERE?
Y-YES...

PUT HIM ON.
WHAT ?!
I'M GOING TO TELL HIM TO WATCH IT IF HE KNOWS WHAT'S GOOD FOR HIM.
TH-THAT WON'T BE NECESSARY!
EVERYTHING'S F-F-FINE!
IF HE PULLS ANYTHING, SCREAM AS LOUD AS YOU CAN.
Y-YOU SHOULD TRUST HIM MORE, AKEMI!
KLIK
YES. YES. TRUST HIM.
THAT WAS AKEMI CALLING TO SAY SHE GOT TO THE HOTEL.
BINK
HUH ?!
HO... HO... HO...
DIDN'T I TELL YOU SHE WAS GOING SKIING ?
NO WAY !
SO... THIS MEANS...
AKEMI WON'T BE HERE ?
THAT'S RIGHT.

LONELY, ISN'T IT?
JUST THE TWO OF US?
YES. ISN'T IT?

JUST THE TWO OF US...
OH! IT'S STARTING!
THE NEW YEAR'S SINGING CONTEST!

THIS IS MY CHANCE!
SHE COULD YELL AND NOBODY WOULD HEAR!

.....
WE VOW TO FIGHT AS BEST WE CAN
INCH INCH

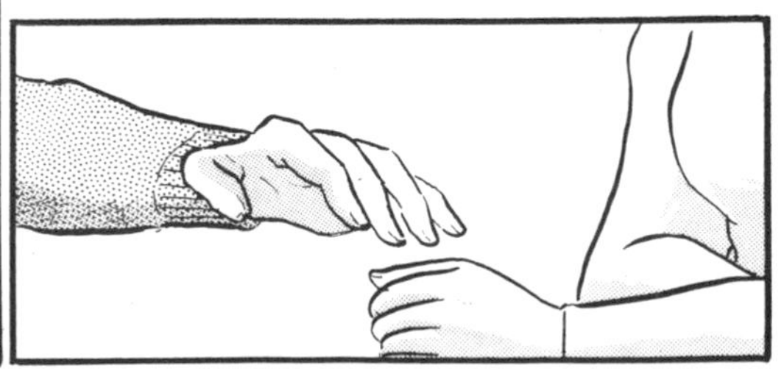

HEY! CAN I GRAB AN ORANGE?
VIP
GLOMP

SAY, IT'S NICE TO HAVE A TV, ISN'T IT?
DO YOU THINK YOU'LL BUY ONE?

I MAY SAVE UP FOR ONE. HEH-HEH.
IT REALLY IS NICE TO HAVE ONE.

UM...CAN YOU SEE ALL RIGHT FROM THERE?
I'M NOT IN YOUR WAY?
NO, NO! I'M FINE!

WHO CARES ABOUT THE LOUSY TV?!
TREMBLE

IN A SINGLE MOVE...
NOW!

THE VOLUME'S TOO LOW.
I'LL PULL HER TO ME!

FOMP

VASH

HER HAND... UNDER THERE... SLOWLY...
INCH INCH

KRAKKLE
OH!
I FORGOT I PUT THE RICE CRACKERS UNDER THERE!
DON'T YOU JUST LOVE RICE CRACKERS?
MUNCH MUNCH MUNCH MUNCH
MUNCH MUNCH MUNCH MUNCH
YEAH. SURE.

NOW, LET ME GET THE NOODLES READY.
I'LL HELP YOU.

NO, PLEASE. JUST WATCH TV.
NO, NO, NO! I'M IMPOSING ON YOU!
PIYO PIYO

BUT THERE'S NOTHING FOR YOU TO DO.
BUT... BUT...
.....
PANT PANT PANT
TON TON
I KNOW! YOU CAN BRING ME THE BOWLS!
UM... THE BOWLS?
BOWLS!
BLAST IT, BLAST IT!
HAVE SOME TEA.
OW. OW. OW.
INCH INCH

RRRING
WHO COULD THAT BE?
WHPP
MRS. ICHINOSE!
WHAT? YOUR GAS VALVE?
I'LL CHECK ON IT RIGHT NOW.
THANKS! BYE!

I'M GOING TO CHECK ROOM 1.
UH-HUH.
CLICK
IT'S NO GOOD. I JUST CAN'T DO IT!
ARRGH!
I WANT TO...I WANT TO...

DAMN IT, I WANT TO DO IT!
BAM
GASP
UM...
YAA!!

UH...DID YOU HEAR WHAT I...
WELL... SORT OF...
I WAS THINKING THAT I REALLY WANT TO SKI.
I REALLY ENVY AKEMI. SKIING, I MEAN.
DON'T YOU ?
OH! SKIING !
AND TO THINK THAT I THOUGHT...
THE WHITE TEAM FOUGHT ITS HARDEST...
BUT THE RED TEAM WOULD NOT BE BEATEN!
SHOULD OLD ACQUAINTANCE BE FORGOT
THIS IS DELICIOUS!
SLURRP
.....
I SHOULD BE GOING.
SO SOON ?
YEAH. THE SHOW'S OVER, SO...
WELL. G'NIGHT.
GOODBYE! GOODBYE!
.....
HE LEFT! JUST LIKE THAT!
CLICK
HE DIDN'T TRY A THING.
HE REALLY IS A PERFECT GENTLEMAN.
AUGHH !
WHAT A COWARD.

TONNNNG
THIS WAS MY ONE AND ONLY CHANCE.
I CHOKED UNDER PRESSURE.
WHY DID I THINK HE WOULD MAKE A MOVE?
TONNNNG
NOT YUSAKU!
HE JUST ISN'T THAT KIND OF GUY!
TONNNNG
I SHOULD'VE... I SHOULD'VE...
OHHHH...
YUSAKU? ARE YOU AWAKE?
TAP TAP
HUH?!
I'M GOING TO SEE IF HE WANTS TO!
I'M GOING TO DO IT!
TONNNG
OH!
KYOKO...!

DO YOU WANT TO COME TO THE TEMPLE WITH ME TO RING IN THE NEW YEAR?
WELL... YEAH!
I'D LOVE TO!
FOR A SECOND THERE, I ACTUALLY EXPECTED TO OPEN THE DOOR AND FIND HER IN A NEGLIGEE.
TONNNNG
BUT KYOKO JUST ISN'T THAT KIND OF GIRL.
I HOPE YOU HAVE A GOOD YEAR.
OH, I WILL. THIS YEAR I'M REALLY GONNA DO IT!

Part Five

"I'll be Back"

OH, YOU ARE?
WELL, OKAY.
SURE, SURE, NO PROBLEM.
AFTER ALL, YOU HAVEN'T SEEN THEM FOR QUITE A WHILE.
CHING
SKEEEK
Yusaku Back
BUSY...?
NO, NO. COME ON IN.

YUSAKU'S COMING BACK TODAY, ISN'T HE?
WELL, I WAS JUST TALKING TO HIM ON THE PHONE...
...AND HE SAYS HE'S GOING TO STAY WITH HIS PAR-ENTS FOR ANOTHER TWO OR THREE DAYS.
OH, YEAH?
YOU MUST BE LONELY, POOR GIRL.
HUH?
SO...I HEAR YOU TWO WERE ALL ALONE ON NEW YEAR'S EVE...
SHKK
N-NOTHING HAPPENED, I'LL HAVE YOU KNOW.
THAT A FACT...? OKAY, BE THAT WAY ABOUT IT, THEN!
IT'S TRUE!
YOU DIDN'T EVEN HOLD HANDS?
CERTAINLY NOT!
IN FACT, HE WAS A PERFECT GENTLE-MAN.
WHEW... IF ANYTHING HAD HAPPENED, IT WOULD HAVE BEEN HALF MY FAULT.
WHADDA YA MEAN, "WHEW"..? IT WOULD'VE BEEN GREAT!

HMM... WONDER WHY HE'S STAYING LONGER.
PROBABLY JUST HOMESICK, DON'T YOU THINK?
MAYBE HE PREFERS MOMMY TO HIS GIRLFRIEND.
YEAH, MAYBE... AFTER ALL, HE *IS* STILL JUST A KID.
OH, COME ON!

HE'S JUST BEING A GOOD SON!
AFTER ALL, HE DIDN'T HAVE A CHANCE TO SEE THEM DURING SUMMER VACATION.
YEAH, WELL, MAYBE.

COMPARED TO LAST YEAR, HE'S A BIT MORE OF A MAN, ISN'T HE?
HIS *BODY* IS, ANYWAY!
ISN'T TWENTY THE PEAK OF A MAN'S SEXUAL DRIVE...?
I CAN'T BELIEVE I HEARD THAT...

AND SHE STILL SAYS NOTHING HAPPENED.
YOU TWO NEVER GIVE UP, DO YOU?
NOT EVEN A NEW YEAR'S KISS AT MIDNIGHT?
NO, WE DID **NOT!!**
WHAK

YUSAKU HERE.
IT ALL STARTED ABOUT THREE DAYS EARLIER...
SIR!
WE REGRET THAT ONCE AGAIN WE FAILED--
YOU DON'T HAVE TO SAY IT!
OBVIOUSLY YOU BLEW THE BIG GAME, OR WE WOULDN'T BE FREEZING OUR BUTTS OFF OUT HERE DURING VACATION!
WE'LL USE OUR ANGER FROM OUR DEFEAT TO FOCUS FOR NEXT YEAR!
THAT'S THE WAY!
YEAH. *WE* DID THAT EVERY YEAR FOR THREE YEARS!
HOPE YOU COLLEGE GUYS CAN SHOW US A THING OR TWO!
YOU GUYS IN SHAPE FOR THIS?
ARE YOU KIDDING ?!
I'M *TOTALLY* OUT OF SHAPE!

YOU MAY NOT BELIEVE IT TO LOOK AT ME... BUT I USED TO PLAY RUGBY IN HIGH SCHOOL.

RUN! RUN!
HEY, LOOK!
NICE SHORTS!
TA TA TA TA TA TOOM

WHAT A STUD I AM!
I WISH KYOKO COULD SEE ME NOW!

WHUMP

AND THREE DAYS LATER...
YEAH, LOOKS LIKE I'LL BE HERE ANOTHER FEW DAYS.
GODAI
CAFE

WELL, MY PARENTS REALLY ENJOY HAVING ME AROUND, Y'KNOW...
HA, HA, HA.
WHAT'S THIS "MY PARENTS ENJOY HAVING ME AROUND" NONSENSE?
CHING
C'MON, GRANNY-- I CAN'T TELL HER THE TRUTH, CAN I?
THINK YOU'RE A REAL "PRETTY BOY," DON'T YOU?
AW, MAN... JUST LOOK AT THIS.
IT'S A PATHETIC SIGHT, TRUE ENOUGH.
WHAT WERE YOU THINKING, PLAYING THAT SILLY GAME WHEN YOU'RE SO OUT OF SHAPE?
MOTHER'S RIGHT... I WAS HOPING YOU'D HELP US OUT IN THE RESTAURANT.
YUSAKU, HOW ABOUT STAYING UNTIL THE 15TH?
WHY?
WELL, THEN YOU COULD BE HERE FOR THE "COMING OF AGE" FESTIVAL.
AW, I TURNED TWENTY A LONG TIME AGO, MOM.
SOON AS THIS EYE LOOKS BETTER, I'M HEADING BACK TO TOKYO.
DON'T YOU MEAN "I'M HEADING BACK TO KYOKO."?
WHO ASKED YOU?
FUMP

OKAY, CLASS, LET'S CALL IT A DAY.
PHEW...
MS. OTONASHI, WOULD YOU JOIN ME FOR A CUP OF COFFEE?
WELL...
TODAY'S THE 8TH...
YUSAKU MIGHT BE COMING BACK...
AW, GO AHEAD--LET THE COACH CHEER YOU UP.
ABOUT WHAT?
SHE'S BEEN MOPING AROUND BECAUSE GODAI HASN'T COME BACK YET.
NO KIDDING...
I SHOULD'VE KNOWN YOU'D SAY SOMETHING LIKE THAT.
WELL, I CAN GO FOR A LITTLE WHILE, ANYWAY.
I HOPE I'M NOT JUST A SUBSTITUTE FOR GODAI.

IT MUST BE NICE TO HAVE A SMALL HOMETOWN TO RETREAT TO.
SO YOU'RE FROM TOKYO?
HOW ABOUT YOU, MS. OTONASHI?
WE WERE ALWAYS MOVING BECAUSE OF MY FATHER'S JOB.
I DON'T REALLY FEEL I CAN CALL ANYWHERE "MY HOMETOWN."
IS IT REALLY TRUE THAT YOU'RE LONELY?
HM?
BECAUSE GODAI'S BEEN AWAY SO LONG.
OH, PLEASE!
DON'T TELL ME YOU TOOK THAT SERIOUSLY?
YOU'VE GOT TO BE KIDDING!
OKAY, OKAY!
ANYWAY, I'M GLAD.
SPARKLE
I'M HOME...

AND YUSAKU STILL ISN'T BACK?
YOU SURE WEREN'T GONE LONG.
WELL, I THOUGHT I'D BETTER BE HERE TO WELCOME HIM BACK, SO I MADE IT QUICK.
WELL, THAT SOUNDS PLAUSIBLE... I GUESS.
IF HE WERE COMING, HE'D PROBABLY CALL FIRST, RIGHT?
MMM... I GUESS YOU'RE RIGHT.
MUCH BETTER.
WON'T BE TOO BAD IF SHE SEES THIS.
YUSAKU! I'VE GOT A DELIVERY FOR YOU TO MAKE!
FIRST TIME HOME IN MONTHS AND ALL YOU DO IS SIT AROUND LIKE A LUMP! GET A MOVE ON!
GEEZ... HE'S WORKIN' ME LIKE A DOG.
THIS IS EXACTLY WHY I DIDN'T WANT TO STAY HERE TOO LONG!

DELIVERY FROM GODAI'S!
MY GOODNESS! IS THAT YOU, YUSAKU?
JUST LOOK AT HOW BIG YOU'VE GOTTEN!
HOW LONG ARE YOU HERE FOR?
I'LL BE GOING BACK TOMORROW.
I'D BETTER REMEMBER TO CALL KYOKO...
WHOOOOSH
TOMORROW I'LL SEE HER AGAIN...
YUSAKU, I MISSED YOU SO MUCH!
I'M BACK, NOW.
I'M SORRY TO LEAVE YOU ALONE FOR SO LONG...
KYOKO !!
YUSAKU !!
SHRANGGG
CIG
URRR
YEEOW! MOM, THAT HURTS!!
SIT STILL OR I'M GOING TO GET THIS MEDICINE ALL OVER YOUR FACE!
GODAI
GODAI
CAFE

SO WHAT ABOUT TOMORROW?
ARE YOU GOING TO TOKYO ?
YEAH, RIGHT. GO BACK LOOKING LIKE THIS?

GOOD HEAVENS, SUCH WHINING! ACT LIKE A MAN!
COME ON... LET ME SEE.

OH, NO!!
HA HA HA
RATS !

RRIINNGG

HELLO ?
OH, YUSAKU !
SO WHEN ARE YOU COMING HOME?

OH...
ANOTHER TWO OR THREE DAYS...?

I DUNNO... MAYBE THREE OR FOUR.
I'LL COME BACK AS SOON AS I CAN, BUT...
...I'M JUST NOT SURE YET.

UM...
IS...IS SOMETHING THE MATTER?

NO, NO...IT'S JUST, Y'KNOW, MY PARENTS WANT ME TO STAY...
HA HA HA
VAIN LITTLE BRAT, ISN'T HE...?

......
CHING
HEY, MS. OTONASHI!
OH, KOZUE.
WHAT'S UP WITH YUSAKU?
HE'S BEEN GONE FOR PRACTICALLY *FOREVER*.
HM?
SUSHI
THAT DUMMY...
WE EVEN HAD A DATE TO SEE A MOVIE ON THE 10TH.
SO YOU DON'T KNOW WHY HE'S STAYING AWAY SO LONG, EITHER.
NOPE.
HE CALLED ME YESTERDAY, BUT HE DIDN'T SAY.
I SEE.
I WONDER WHAT'S WRONG...
I SURE MISS HIM...

FFFH
SKSSH
SKSSH
SURE IS COLD...
FTAP
FTAP
OH!
BTAM
I HOPE HE'S COMING HOME SOON...

Yusaku
Back
12 13 14

SKSSH
SKSSH

BTAM
BTAM
OH... JUST THE WIND.

5

SKSSH
5

NOK
NOK

5

SKSSH
MAN, THE KID'S REALLY LATE... SCHOOL'S ALREADY STARTED!
HE MUST BE REALLY COMFORTABLE AT HOME, EH?
HMPH. HE'S PROBABLY JUST HOMESICK.
I MEAN, AFTER ALL, HE IS JUST A KID.
WAIT A SEC!
"AFTER ALL, HE DIDN'T HAVE A CHANCE TO SEE THEM DURING SUMMER VACATION."
YEAH..."HE'S JUST BEING A GOOD SON!"
DID I SAY THAT...?
THIS REALLY IS ANNOYING.
I HAVE RENT TO COLLECT, YOU KNOW!
HECK, RENT ISN'T EVEN DUE FOR ANOTHER TEN DAYS!
SHE'S REALLY PISSED, ISN'T SHE?
WHISPER
WHISPER
WHISPER
YEAH... MIGHT BE KINDA RISKY TO TEASE HER RIGHT NOW.
IS THAT WHAT THEY CALL A "STAGE WHISPER"..?!

DARN IT ALL, ANYWAY!
JUST WHAT IS THAT DUMMY DOING ?!
AS IT HAPPENS, "THAT DUMMY" IS ALMOST HOME.
GEEZ... BOOTED OUT OF MY OWN PARENTS' HOUSE.

HE'S HOPELESS.
I MEAN, IF HE'S GOING TO HANG AROUND UP THERE, AT LEAST HE OUGHT TO HAVE THE DECENCY TO CALL ME!
BTAM
HEY, AIN'T THAT THE KID ?
JUST THE WIND.

I'LL CHECK IT OUT...
IF IT WAS HIM, HE'D SAY "I'M HOME."
ARE YOU COMING ?
WHAT'S YOUR PROBLEM ?
YOU'RE BEING REAL OBSTINATE ABOUT THIS.
....
HEY, YUSAKU, WHAT THE HELL HAVE YOU BEEN DOIN'?
WELL, UH, Y'KNOW...SOME STUFF...

BWA HA HA HEE HEE HA HA
HE'S BACK!
HEY, KYOKO, COME ON!! HURRY!
HE... HE'S BACK!
I...I CAN'T COME RIGHT NOW.
HEY, KYOKO, C'MON!
SSHHH
WHAT WAS THAT?!
SO WHAT DIFFERENCE WILL A WHILE LONGER MAKE?!
WHAT KINDA TALK IS THAT? YOU HAVEN'T SEEN HER FOR WEEKS!!
DON'T BOTHER HER--I HAVE TO PUT MY LUGGAGE AWAY, ANYHOW.
HONESTLY, WHAT--
HURRY, HURRY!
COME ON, KID, COME ON!

HEY.
WHAT IN THE...?
DOES HE THINK THOSE ARE COOL?
JUST WHO DOES HE THINK HE...
TA-DAAAA!!
FWIP
HEY, YOU STUPID--
OH, NO!
....
WELL, DEAR, I'M CERTAINLY GLAD YOU'RE BACK.
WE HAVEN'T SEEN HER LAUGH LIKE THAT FOR AGES.
MMRFF... HNGG... HMPHH...
I DUNNO... YOU FIGURE THAT COUNTS AS LAUGHING...?
MMPH...
MMPH... MMPPH...
DAMN IT... I KNEW I SHOULDA STAYED FOR A FEW MORE DAYS...

Part Six

Kyoko Baby and Mr. Soichiro

KACHING
FINALS ARE OVER!
CONGRATULATIONS!
ROCK AND ROLL!
MAN, I'M GONNA DO SOME SERIOUS DRINKING!
HEE HEE HEE
HAW HAW HAW
THINK YOU'LL PASS?
I KNOW I'LL PASS OUT!
HEY, YOU GOIN' HOME FOR THE BREAK?
BEER SAKE
WHO, ME?
NAW... I WAS JUST BACK FOR NEW YEAR'S.
THEY'RE PROBABLY SICK OF ME.

NO KIDDIN'... HEY, DRINK UP!
HUH?
I'M GOING HOME... JUST FOR A WEEK OR SO, ANYWAY.
OH, YEAH?
C'MON-- HAVE ANOTHER!
??
BEER SAKE

SO WHATCHA DOIN' OVER THE BREAK?
TRAVEL A BIT?
NAW... GOTTA WORK.
YA

RIGHT ON!
WHAP

C'MON, SUCK 'EM UP!
TONIGHT, THE BOOZE IS ON ME!
BLUP BLUP BLUP
OH, YEAH? GREAT, THANKS!

I FIGURED SOMETHING WAS UP, AND SURE ENOUGH...

"CAT"...?
WHAT THE HELL ?!

YOU DON'T KNOW WHAT A CAT IS?
FOUR LEGS, TAIL, GOES "MEOW."
THAT'S NOT THE QUESTION, AND YOU KNOW IT!

YOU PROMISED, ALL RIGHT.
YEAH, WELL, I DON'T.
RANMA 1/2
I MEAN, WHEN DID I PROMISE TO TAKE CARE OF YOUR CAT?
LAST NIGHT.
DON'T TELL ME YOU DON'T REMEMBER.
DO YOU REMEMBER THAT I HAD TO PAY FOR IT ALL, YOU LUSH?
I REMEMBER ONE THING--YOU WERE REALLY POURING THE BOOZE INTO ME LAST NIGHT, WEREN'T YOU?
I'M NOT ALLOWED TO KEEP PETS IN MY APARTMENT, ANYWAY!
IN YOU GO, GIRL!
MEOW
HERE SHE COMES, NOW.
MEOW
I WAS PLASTERED!
HEY, PAL, YOU SWORE YOU'D DO IT--"LEAVE HER WITH ME," YOU SAID!
DAMMIT, SAKAMOTO, THAT WAS A DIRTY TRICK!

OKAY, KYOKO BABY, GO SAY HELLO TO UNCLE GODAI.
URK!
"KYOKO BABY!"..?!
"YEP. AS SOON AS I SAID THAT NAME, LAST NIGHT..."
WHAT?! WHY DIDN'T YOU SAY SO IN THE FIRST PLACE?!
LEAVE HER WITH ME!
WELL...? YOU GONNA DENY IT?
NO WAY OUT...
WHY WOULD YOU NAME A CAT "KYOKO BABY," ANYWAY?
'CAUSE MY FAVORITE STAR IS KYOKO MANO! OH, BABY!
RANM 1/2
WELL, IT'S GONNA BE A BIT OF A PROBLEM WHEN I CALL HER. MY APARTMENT MANAGER'S NAME IS "KYOKO," TOO.
SO WHAT DO YOU WANT ME TO DO ABOUT IT? YOU GOTTA CALL HER "KYOKO BABY" OR SHE WON'T RESPOND.

YUSAKU!
IF YOU'RE GOING TO SPEND THE NIGHT SOMEWHERE ELSE, THE LEAST YOU CAN DO IS CALL ME!
PIYO PIYO
SORRY ABOUT THAT.
I WAS UP HALF THE NIGHT WAITING, WITH THE FRONT DOOR UNLOCKED!
I'M REAL SORRY... IT WON'T--
SKF SKF
PIYO PIYO
NO! DON'T--!
MEW?

....!

ER...DON'T WORRY...I'LL BE SURE TO CALL YOU NEXT TIME.

CANNED CAT FOOD...
...AND DRY.

NOW, FOR A CAT BOX.
GUESS I'LL TEAR UP SOME NEWSPAPERS AND PUT 'EM IN HERE...

OKAY, KYOKO BABY...
THIS'LL BE YOUR NEW CAT BOX--

FWAP
KYOKO BABY!

BTAM

ER...HI. WHAT'S UP?

YOU JUST CALLED ME, DIDN'T YOU?

NOK NOK NOK

HELLO? YUSAKU?!

I DON'T REALLY UNDERSTAND WHAT YOU MEANT BY SAYING I WAS HIDING...

SO WHAT'S THE PROBLEM?

YOU SAY I CALLED YOU...?

OF COURSE YOU DID! I CLEARLY HEARD YOU CALL "KYOKO BABY"!!
HA, HA... C'MON, WOULD I EVER DARE TO CALL YOU "KYOKO BABY"...?
WELL...YOU SHOULDN'T, BUT...
YOU MUST BE HEARING THINGS.
THEN YOU DON'T NEED ME.
UM... NO.
.....
KYOKO BABY...
SKSSH
MEW
COME· ON...
I PROMISE I WON'T HIT YOU AGAIN.
OH, HO...
....!

MR. YOTSU--!
SHH!

MEOW.
MEOW!

KYOKO BABY, COME TO MY ARMS...
I DON'T LIKE THE WAY YOU SAY THAT!

WHY? THE CAT'S NAME IS "KYOKO BABY," IS IT NOT?
YEAH, BUT YOUR VOICE DIDN'T SOUND LIKE IT WAS CALLING A CAT!

SHE'S VERY CUTE.
BONK
SMAK

THIS IS ONLY A CAT, GODAI.
I KNOW THAT!

HMM...IT APPEARS TO BE A FEMALE.
DON'T LOOK AT THAT!
PERHAPS YOU SHOULD NOT BE KEEPING A CAT HERE.
IT'S JUST FOR A WEEK.

PERHAPS I SHOULD INFORM THE MANAGER...
I SAID IT'S JUST FOR A WEEK!!

IT IS AGAINST THE RULES.
....

ALL RIGHT... ONE DINNER.
I'LL MAKE SAKAMOTO PAY ME BACK LATER.
BUT YOU HAVE TO KEEP YOUR MOUTH SHUT.
A HUMBLE MEAL SHALL SUFFICE.
IT IS MERELY THAT I FIND MYSELF TEMPORARILY SHORT OF FUNDS.

HEY, I WANNA SEE THE KITTY-CAT!

I ASSUMED THAT YOU MEANT THAT ONLY THE MANAGER MUST REMAIN UNAWARE.
WHERE'S THE KITTY?
HERE, PUSS-PUSS!
DAMMIT, YOTSUYA!

AHA, THERE YOU ARE!

WHITEY !
SNOWY !
MARSHMALLOW!

'EY, WHAT'S ITS STUPID NAME ?!
SHH! SHH!

SO WHAT'S THE LIL' RASCAL'S NAME ?
.....

BLUP
BLUP
BLUP

MMM... SMELLS GOOD.

"KYOKO BABY"?!
Splttt

GEEZ, AKEMI! DIDJA HAVE TO YELL?!
HEY, I WAS SURPRISED, OKAY?!
TM TM TM
AKEMI? AKEMI!
NOK NOK
EEP!
ARE YOU OKAY?
AKEMI!
NOK NOK
GO TELL HER SOMETHING!
I'M A LOUSY LIAR.
I DON'T CARE! JUST TELL HER SOMETHING SHE'LL BELIEVE!
WHATEVER YOU SAY...
OHH...MS. OTONASHI...
THANK GOD YOU'RE H-HERE...
MY GOODNESS! WHAT HAPPENED?!
IT...IT'S ALL RIGHT... IT'S JUST...
...YUSAKU SUDDENLY JUMPED ON ME!
HE DID WHAT?!?
WHUMP

YUSAKU, HOW COULD YOU?!
IT'S A LIE! A LIE!!
WHAM

SCARY LADY, ISN'T SHE?
DAMN YOU, AKEMI!
HONESTLY, YUSAKU-- HAVE YOU NO SHAME?!

HEY, I WARNED YOU I WAS LOUSY AT LYING, DIDN'T I? HUH?
THERE! YOU HEAR THAT? IT'S A LIE!

WHY WOULD SHE LIE ABOUT SOMETHING LIKE THAT?

DO YOU GET SOME SORT OF SICK THRILL OUT OF TEASING ME?
IT'S NOT LIKE THAT, I SWEAR!
I'M FOR BED.

RATS...
IT'S HARDLY DRIED AT ALL.

MEW?
THIS IS ALL YOUR FAULT, YOU LITTLE BEAST!
MEOW
....
THERE WERE NO PROBLEMS FOR THREE OR FOUR DAYS AFTER THAT...
KNGH KRNGH
I STARTED GETTING PRETTY ATTACHED TO HER...
KYOKO BABY...
HEY, YUSAKU-- PHONE.
NOK NOK
WHO IS IT ?
A MAN, UNFORTUNATELY.
BTAM
VWIP

YO, SAKAMOTO.
KYOKO BABY? SHE'S FINE.
WHAT? WHAT DID HE CALL THE MANAGER?
SHE SLEEPS IN MY ARMS EVERY NIGHT.
YEAH, SHE JUST SLIPS INTO MY BED WITHOUT ME EVEN REALIZING IT.
I...I DON'T BELIEVE THIS!
THE TWO OF THEM ARE SLEEPING TOGETHER?!
MARKET
KYOKO!
OH, MRS. ICHINOSE.
YOU'RE LOOKING LIKE THE CAT THAT ATE THE CANARY... WHY?

'WHO WOULD HAVE THOUGHT... STILL WATERS RUN DEEP, I GUESS.
COME ON... WHAT'S UP?
OH, I JUST HEARD SOMETHING INTEREST-ING.
OVER-HEARD IT, ACTUALLY.
I HAVE TO ADMIT IT'S A RELIEF.
I MEAN KNOWING YOU'RE A NORMAL, HEALTHY WOMAN.
WHAT?!
I AM NOT SLEEPING WITH YUSAKU GODAI!!
SHH!

KYOKO BABY!
WHERE ARE YOU, KYOKO BABY?

KYOKO BABY!
KYO-KO BABY!

MAN, WHAT A NIGHTMARE.
C'MON, KYOKO BABY, WHERE ARE YOU?!

I'M RIGHT HERE.

NOW TELL ME ABOUT HOW I SNEAK INTO YOUR BED.

YEESH.

THIS HAD BETTER BE GOOD, MR. GODAI!!
LET ME EXPLAIN--
WELL... UH...
YOU SAID, "SHE SLEEPS IN MY ARMS EVERY NIGHT."
THAT'S WHAT YOU SAID, ALL RIGHT.
MRS. ICHINOSE !!
ISN'T THIS CAT FOOD...?
WELL, UH...
...SMELLS LIKE--
SAY... THIS ROOM...
WAIT A SEC! I FORGOT-SHE'S DISAPPEARED!
IT'S AGAINST THE RULES, SO I DIDN'T WANT TO...
IF IT WAS A CAT, WHY DIDN'T YOU JUST TELL ME?!
SO THIS "KYOKO BABY" IS A...
YEAH.

AW, THAT'S ALL RIGHT.
I'M REAL SORRY ABOUT THIS...
KYOKO BABY!
KYOKO BABY!
??
WURF?
THIS IS SO HUMILIATING!
KYOKO BABY!
KYOKO BABY!
HEY, MS. OTONASHI, C'MERE, C'MERE!
OH, KENTARO.
"KYOKO BABY" AND "MR. SOICHIRO." HOW PERFECT!
HEY, YUSAKU, IF YOU'RE LOOKIN' FOR THE MANAGER, SHE'S RIGHT HERE!
KYOKO BABY...!
KYOKO BABY!
AH!
KINDA FUNNY, ISN'T IT?

Part Seven

A Family Affair

SUNDAY
LAUNDROMAT
KTAK KTAK
KTAK KTAK
.....
GUESS I'LL JUST HAVE TO DRY THEM AT HOME.
NICE AND SUNNY TODAY, ANYWAY.
BUT THAT BALCONY BY THE CLOTHES-LINE SCARES THE BEJABBERS OUT OF ME...
I WISH KYOKO WOULD JUST CALL A CON-TRACTOR AND GET THE THING FIXED.

HEY... WHAT'S THIS GUY UP TO?
SO, THERE ARE YOUNG MEN LIVING HERE, TOO.
THIS IS EVEN WORSE THAN I THOUGHT...
HUH... WEIRD...
MAYBE HE'S THINKING OF RENTING... NAW, NO WAY.
YEAH... ALL THE DRYERS WERE BEING USED.
DRYING YOUR STUFF ON THE LINE TODAY? THAT'S UNUSUAL.
THAT GUY GIVES ME THE CREEPS, JUST STANDING AND STARING LIKE THAT.
TUMP TUMP

WHOA! NOT THERE!
HUH ?!

THAT'S FUNNY... I THOUGHT THE FIRST BOARD WAS THE ONLY ROTTEN ONE.
BOY, YOU'RE NOT UP HERE MUCH, ARE YOU ?
KREEK

THIS OLD DUMP IS FALLING APART AT THE SEAMS.
SAY...YOU THINK THIS THING WILL HOLD BOTH OF US ?
KREEK
SIGH...WHEN I MOVE INTO A NICE NEW APARTMENT...
YOU'RE MOVING ?!

DON'T GET YOUR HOPES UP, SONNY BOY.
HUH ?

AW, I DIDN'T MEAN IT LIKE THAT.
MY HUSBAND DOESN'T MAKE ENOUGH FOR US TO MOVE, ANYWAY.

I'M STUCK HERE, UNLIKE SOME STUDENTS WHO JUST HANG AROUND BECAUSE THE MANAGER'S GORGEOUS.
WHATEVER YOU SAY.
FWAP

JEEZ... STILL THERE.
"SOME WEIRDO"...?
YEAH, THIS FAT, CREEPY-LOOKING MIDDLE-AGED GUY.
HE'S BEEN STANDING OUT THERE FOR ALMOST AN HOUR.
I'D BETTER GO TAKE A LOOK.
KYOKO, WAIT!
YOU OUGHT TO BE MORE CAREFUL--WHAT IF HE'S SOME KIND OF PER-VERT OR PSYCHO?
OH, COME ON!
I DUNNO... MAYBE WE OUGHT TO JUST CALL THE COPS.
DON'T WORRY.
ULP!
VWIP
MAISON IKKOKU
I DON'T SEE ANYONE, YUSAKU...
HUH? THAT'S WEIRD.

HEY !!
ALL RIGHT, YOU !!
JUST WHAT THE HELL ARE YOU DOING ?!
URK!
PIYO
VOOOM
EH ?
HEY, YOU!
NOW DON'T TELL ME *THAT'S* NOT SUSPICIOUS!
PIYO
PROBABLY A BURGLAR OR ARSONIST.
D-DID HE REALLY LOOK THAT BAD?
PIYO PIYO
WORSE THAN THAT! HE LOOKED LIKE A PERVERT! LIKE A RAPIST!
YOU THINK SO?
YOU SHOULD'VE SEEN HIM, KYOKO! HE WAS TOTALLY *DEPRAVED*!
Y-YOU DON'T SAY.
NEXT TIME HE SHOWS HIS UGLY PERVOID MUG AROUND HERE, I'M CALLING THE COPS!
UM... YUSAKU...

THAT WAS MY DAD.
KLONG
.....
YOU'RE JOKING, RIGHT ?
I'D RECOGNIZE THAT OLD COAT ANYWHERE.
.....
A HA HA HEH...
I WAS JUST KIDDING... ACTUALLY, HE LOOKED LIKE A GREAT OLD GUY.
I'M SORRY, YUSAKU.
I CAN'T BLAME YOU FOR GETTING THE WRONG IDEA, THE WAY HE WAS SNEAKING AROUND LIKE A CRIMINAL.

I FIGURE THERE'S MORE TO THIS THAN MEETS THE EYE...
BUT I CAN'T QUITE GET A GRIP ON WHAT IT MIGHT BE.
SAY, KOZUE... HAVE YOU EVER FOUGHT WITH YOUR FATHER?
MM ?
GEE, THAT'S A FUNNY QUESTION... WHY?
AW, NO REAL REASON. JUST CURIOUS, THAT'S ALL.
I WAS JUST, Y'KNOW, WONDERING WHAT IT'S LIKE BETWEEN FATHER AND DAUGHTER.
HMM...
I'D HAVE TO SAY DAD DOESN'T REALLY KNOW HOW TO RELATE TO ME.
HE'S KIND OF... UPTIGHT.
UPTIGHT, HUH?
LET'S SAY... FOR EXAMPLE...
SOME GIRL GOT MARRIED AGAINST HER FATHER'S WISHES.
YEAH ?

WHAT DO YOU THINK HE WOULD DO?
OH, DON'T WORRY! MY DAD WOULDN'T BE A PROBLEM AT ALL!

I'M SURE HE'D GET ALONG WITH YOU JUST FINE, YUSAKU!
W-WHAT ?!

I MEAN, DAD ALWAYS SAID IF I GOT A BOYFRIEND I OUGHTA BRING HIM HOME FOR SURE.
HE WANTS TO MAKE SURE IT'S SOMEONE HE CAN TRUST HIS DAUGHTER WITH, HE SAYS.
YEAH, OKAY, BUT WHAT IF HE CHECKS THE GUY OUT AND DOESN'T LIKE HIM?

WELL, I GUESS THE FACT WE'RE BOTH STILL SO YOUNG MIGHT BE A PROBLEM.
WHAT IS SHE TALKING ABOUT ?

MAYBE I SHOULD CALL...

SHKKKK
CHIK
CHIK
CHIK

.....

ON SECOND THOUGHT...
CHING

I CAN HEAR IT ALL NOW--
"COME BACK HOME, DEAR! WE'LL FIND YOU A NICE NEW HUSBAND!"

RRIINNGG

.....
RRIINNGG
HELLO ?
RRII-
OH, IT'S YOU, MOTHER.
SO. FATHER TELLS ME HE DIDN'T GET A CHANCE TO SPEAK TO YOU.

HE TOLD ME WHAT HAPPENED, BUT--
HE WHAT ?!
ONE OF MY TENANTS EVEN THOUGHT HE WAS SOME KIND OF CRIMINAL!
I THOUGHT I'D DIE OF EMBARRASSMENT!
DADDY, REALLY!
AND YOU TOLD ME SHE WASN'T HOME!

WHAT'S THIS ALL ABOUT, ANYWAY ?
3 4 5 6
10 11 12 13
16 17 18 19
I'D RATHER NOT TALK ABOUT IT OVER THE PHONE.
WHY DON'T YOU COME BY FOR DINNER NEXT SUNDAY ?
WELL, WHY NOT?
YOU DIDN'T EVEN COME HOME FOR NEW YEAR'S!
AHEM!

HMM.
CHING.

ALL RIGHT, LET'S HEAR IT.
WHY DID YOU RUN AWAY?
WHAT'S THE BIG DEAL...? I SAW THE DAMN APARTMENT.
THAT'S **NOT** WHY YOU WENT THERE!!
IT'S YOUR PIGHEADED ATTITUDE THAT'S KEEPING OUR DAUGHTER FROM COMING BACK HOME!
OH, YEAH? WHY?
AFTER THE WAY YOU FOUGHT HER MARRIAGE TOOTH AND NAIL...
...YOU CAN'T EXPECT HER JUST TO FORGIVE YOU.
I WAS ONLY THINKING OF KYOKO'S WELFARE.
AND THE FACT IS, SOICHIRO DIED ALMOST IMMEDIATELY, DIDN'T HE? RIGHT?!
SHE WOULD HAVE BEEN FAR BETTER OFF WITH SOMEONE YOUNG AND STRONG.
FWAP
HMPH
MUST YOU GO ON AND ON ABOUT SOMETHING THAT'S OVER AND DONE WITH?!
IF YOU DON'T STOP BEING SUCH A STUBBORN OLD MULE I'LL DIVORCE YOU!
BAM
NOW, RITSUKO...

AND SO, THE NEXT SUNDAY...
TAKAMINE HEIGHTS
-SIGHH-
OH, BROTHER...
HOW AM I GOING TO HANDLE THIS...?
JUDGING FROM THE WAY DAD ACTED THE OTHER DAY, I'D SAY HE'S STILL MAD AT ME.
WELL, HE CAN'T STAY MAD IF I SMILE AT HIM.

TINK
I'LL SMILE AND SAY--
"HI THERE, DADDY"...!
SHK
WH-WHY, HELLO, HONEY!
......
HELLO, MOTHER.
OH, YOU FOUND HER?
BUMPED INTO HER AT THE ELEVATOR.
YOUR FATHER WAS ALL IN A FLAP-- "WHERE IS THAT GIRL?"
YOU WANT ME TO WHAT?!
QUIT MY JOB AT MAISON IKKOKU?
TO PUT IT BLUNTLY, YES.
CHIK

THAT RUN-DOWN OLD APARTMENT HOUSE IS NO PLACE FOR A FINE YOUNG GIRL LIKE YOU.
WHAT A THING TO SAY!
THAT "RUN-DOWN OLD APARTMENT HOUSE" IS ***MY*** RESPONSIBILITY, DADDY!
IT'S NOT A MATTER OF WHAT THE PLACE LOOKS LIKE, KYOKO.
THE BUILDING IS OWNED BY SOICHIRO'S FAMILY, ISN'T IT?
WHETHER IT'S YOUR JOB OR NOT...
IT'S JUST NOT HEALTHY TO KEEP SUCH A CLOSE CON-NECTION WITH THE FAMILY OF YOUR LATE HUSBAND.
SURELY YOU CAN SEE THAT.
NO, I CAN'T.
AND BESIDES, LIVING UNDER THE SAME ROOF WITH A YOUNG MAN, REGARDLESS OF WHETHER OR NOT HE'S A TENANT--
"YOUNG MAN"...?
DO YOU MEAN ***YUSAKU***?
HIS NAME DOESN'T MATTER!

MEN WON'T MARRY A WIDOW IF SHE ISN'T A VIRGIN!
DADDY, YOU'RE NOT MAKING ANY SENSE.
HMPH. AND WHO WAS SAYING SHE SHOULD HAVE MARRIED SOMEONE "YOUNG AND STRONG"...?

KYOKO, COME HOME.
THAT'S IMPOSSIBLE.
LISTEN. LET ME MAKE ONE THING VERY CLEAR. I'M NOT WORKING AS THE MANAGER OUT OF ANY SENSE OF OBLIGATION TO THE OTONASHI FAMILY.

I'M WORKING THERE BECAUSE I LIKE IT.
CASE CLOSED, DISCUSSION OVER.
KYOKO, YOU...!
BAM

YOU'D BETTER JUST BE A GOOD GIRL AND DO WHAT YOUR PARENTS TELL YOU!
RRG!
IF YOU DON'T WANT ME TO LIVE MY OWN LIFE, THEN MAYBE WE SHOULD STOP COM-MUNICATING COMPLETELY!
NOW, KYOKO...
BAM

SUCH A STUBBORN CHILD. I CAN'T *IMAGINE* WHERE YOU GET IT FROM!

IN ANY CASE, YOU *WILL* QUIT YOUR JOB.

I WILL *NOT*!
I'M NOT LISTENING!
KYOKO! SIT LIKE A LADY!

"RUN-DOWN OLD APARTMENT BUILDING," EH?

WHAT DOES *HE* KNOW!
THIS IS MY *HOME*.

I'D BETTER GET UP EARLY TOMORROW.
THERE'S A LOT OF WORK TO DO!

BAM BAM
BAM BAM
OH, GREAT! YOU'RE FINALLY FIXING IT!
TUMP TUMP
YES, BUT IT'S JUST A QUICK FIX.
NEED A HAND?
THAT'S ALL RIGHT.
I WANT TO DO IT MYSELF.
YOU'RE CRAZY.
BAM BAM
SHE'S RIGHT! THAT WHOLE BALCONY IS ROTTEN.
HOW'S THAT?
WELL, IT OUGHT TO HOLD FOR A WHILE, ANYWAY.
THUD
THUD
Phew...
WHOA! DON'T--

WHA-?!
KYOKO!
KRAK
I-I'LL CALL A CONTRACTOR TODAY.
WHUDOO
MIGHT NOT BE THE WORST IDEA...
KRAK

SO WHAT IF THIS PLACE IS A LITTLE RUN-DOWN?
AT LEAST THE TENANTS ARE GOOD PEOPLE!
WOW, NO KIDDING? HER AND GODAI WERE MAKING OUT ON THE BALCONY?
YOU BET--AND IN BROAD DAYLIGHT!
EEK!
TSK TSK
....
WELL, AT LEAST THEY'RE GOOD ABOUT PAYING THEIR RENT...
EXCUSE ME, MADAM.
I MUST HUMBLY REQUEST THAT YOU WAIT A SHORT TIME FOR THIS MONTH'S RENT.
....
WILL THAT BE POSSIBLE?
OH, ALL RIGHT...BUT ONLY FOR A LITTLE WHILE.
I DON'T BELIEVE THIS.
IT'S LIKE THEY'RE OUT TO GET ME!
hff hff

BUT I'M NOT GIVING UP!
AFTER ALL, I OUGHT TO BE USED TO THIS SORT OF THING, RIGHT?
BOWF
COME HERE AND OBSERVE.
SNFF SNFF
I'LL NEVER GIVE UP THIS JOB, NO MATTER WHAT.
NOT AS LONG AS MAISON IKKOKU STILL STANDS.
HEY! THOSE ARE TERMITES!!
SURE LOOKS LIKE IT.
THAT'S IT FOR THIS JOINT, THEN.
.....
KTONK

Part Eight

The Big Announcement

BAM BAM BAM BAM
SKSSH SKSSH SKSSH SKSSH
OH, MAN... WHAT'S ALL THE RACKET?
SHKK SHKK
YUH... WHUB'S UB?
HEY, CHECK OUT THE CUTIE!
WHAT'S YOUR PROBLEM?
FLIP FLAP

ALL RIGHT-- FINALLY FIXING THE BALCONY, HUH ?
AND THE EXTERMINATORS ARE OUTSIDE SPRAYING THE TERMITES, TOO.
KYOKO SAID TO TELL HER IF THERE'S ANYTHING ELSE YOU WANT REPAIRED.
NO KIDDIN' ?
SHKK SHKK
I WANT THAT DAMN HOLE IN MY WALL FIXED.
I'LL GO ASK HER.
.....
YOU BETTER MOVE IT, BUDDY.
ALAS, I CANNOT.
MR. GODAI, IT IS APPARENT THAT YOU HAVE NO HEART.
WHY'S THAT ?

THAT INTER-ROOM ORIFICE IS OUR PORTAL OF COMMUNICATIONS.
TO BE PERFECTLY HONEST, I CAN DO WITHOUT "COMMUNICATION" WITH YOU.
DON'T YOU TWO HAVE SOMETHING BETTER TO DO?
I SPENT MUCH TIME TO CONSTRUCT THAT PORTAL.
IT'S AN INVASION OF MY PRIVACY.
THEN YOU INSIST ON FILLING IT?
YOU BET.
SOMETIMES, IN THE STILL OF NIGHT, I HEAR THE VOICE OF GODAI...
"HMM? WHAT'S THIS?" I SAY.
I PRICK UP MY EARS...
"AHH... KYOKO..."
INDEED, THOSE ARE HIS WORDS.
HIS BREATHING IS HEAVY...
YOTSUYA !!

WHATEVER COULD HE BE DOING AS HE CALLS THE MANAGER'S NAME LATE AT NIGHT ?
I WONDER...
WHAT I DO IN MY ROOM IS MY BUSINESS !
MAN, WHAT A SAD CASE... POOR KID.
YEAH, HEART-BREAKING.
PERHAPS IT WOULD BE BEST IF I WERE TO TELL THE MANAGER.
GO AHEAD !

"THE LAD DOTH PROTEST TOO MUCH, METHINKS."
"WE WILL HAVE ALL SUCH OFFENDERS SO CUT OFF." HA!
THIS AIN'T MASTERPIECE THEATRE, YOU KNOW!
YEAH! THIS IS WAY BETTER !
I BELIEVE YOU UNDER-ESTIMATE ME, YOUNG MAN.
AHEM..."GODAI IS USING THE MANAGER AS FODDER FOR HIS DISGUSTING EROTIC FANTASIES!"
YOU REALLY THINK SHE CAN HEAR YOU ALL THE WAY FROM OUTSIDE ?
.....

NO, BUT HOW ABOUT FROM HALFWAY UP THE STAIRS?
. . . . .
. . . . .

GIVING UP?
THUD THUD
YUSAKU...
Y-Y-YES ?
I'VE TALKED TO THE PLASTERERS, SO PLEASE GET YOUR ROOM READY.

I'VE BEEN THINKING FOR QUITE A WHILE THAT I SHOULD FIX THE WALL IN ROOM 5.
BUT, MADAM...

BUT MADAM, YOU'RE CHANGING THE SUBJECT.
WHAT WE SHOULD BE TALKING ABOUT AT THIS TIME IS GODAI'S DISGUSTING--
IF I FIX THE WALL, YOU WON'T HAVE TO LISTEN TO *ANYTHING*, WILL YOU ?!

NOW, LET'S SEE... DOES ANYTHING ELSE NEED TO BE REPAIRED?
THIS OLD PLACE STILL HAS A LOT OF GOOD YEARS LEFT IN IT.
ESPECIALLY SINCE WE CAUGHT THE TERMITES EARLY.
RRIINNGG
HELLO... ?
RRII-
....
OH, IT'S YOU, MOTHER.
"OH, IT'S YOU"...
NICE WAY TO TALK TO YOUR OWN MOTHER!
I DISCUSSED EVERYTHING WITH YOUR FATHER.
NOW, ABOUT YOU QUITTING YOUR JOB--

HOLD IT.
I TOLD YOU, I'M **NOT** QUITTING.
WELL, THEN, WE'LL JUST HAVE TO TALK TO YOUR EMPLOYER DIRECTLY.
DON'T YOU DARE !!
....
THIS IS FOR YOUR OWN GOOD, KYOKO.
IF YOU SAY **ONE WORD** TO THE OTONASHI FAMILY ABOUT THIS, I'LL... I'LL...
I'LL DISOWN YOU !!
KACHINGG
NICE WAY TO TALK TO YOUR OWN DAUGHTER!
HOW **DARE** SHE SPEAK TO ME THAT WAY?!
HOW **DARE** SHE SPEAK TO ME THAT WAY?!

WHAT'S GOTTEN INTO YOU THESE DAYS?
RUNNING AROUND LIKE A MAD FOOL, FIXING UP THE BUILDING...
IT'S JUST MY JOB, MRS. ICHINOSE.
hff hff
YOU MAKE IT SOUND LIKE I HAVEN'T BEEN WORKING UP TILL NOW.
SURE, BUT OUT OF THE BLUE LIKE THIS...

I FORGOT TO BUY SUGAR.
OOPS!
WELL, NO, I DIDN'T MEAN--

YOU GO ON BACK WITHOUT ME.
I'D BETTER TAKE MR. SOICHIRO FOR HIS WALK WHILE I'M AT IT.
BYE, THEN.

.....

I SAY, GODAI...

YOU ARE INDEED CLEANING YOUR ROOM WELL.
ONE MIGHT THINK YOU WERE PREPARING TO MOVE.
I SAY, GODAI!
HOW SAD...HE DESPISES ME.
PERHAPS YOU ARE THE TYPE WHO HOLDS A GRUDGE FOR ALL ETERNITY...?
BE REASONABLE-- THIS IS, INDEED, NOT THE FIRST TIME YOU HAVE BEEN HUMILI-ATED IN FRONT OF THE MANAGER.
.....
SURELY YOU REMEMBER HOW TO SPEAK.
I AM FINDING IT DIFFICULT TO CARRY BOTH SIDES OF THIS CONVER-SATION.

....
....
NOW SHE THINKS I'M SOME KIND OF SEX-CRAZED ADOLESCENT PERVERT...
I...I CAN'T FACE HER AGAIN.
KYOKO...
IF YOU WISH PRIVACY FOR YOUR DISGUSTING ACTS, JUST--
DO I HAVE TO BE DOING IT ***EVERY TIME*** I CALL KYOKO'S NAME?! HUH?! ***DO I?!***
MY JOY IS BOUNDLESS--HE SPOKE TO ME.

EXCUSE ME...IS ANYONE HOME?

I AM KYOKO'S MOTHER.

OH, YEAH?

I'VE COME TO PAY MY REGARDS TO HER TENANTS.

"PAY YOUR REGARDS"...?

WHATEVER IS GOING ON?

BEATS ME...

I WOULD LIKE TO THANK YOU ALL FOR BEING SO KIND TO MY DAUGHTER FOR ALL THESE YEARS.

IT WAS NOTHING.

AS OF TODAY, KYOKO OTONASHI...
...IS PERMANENTLY RETIRING FROM HER POSITION AS MANAGER OF THE MAISON IKKOKU.

THIS IS JUST A SMALL GIFT TO REPAY YOUR KINDNESS.
PLEASE EAT IT TOGETHER AND ENJOY IT.
SLAM

MY GOSH... WHAT A SHOCK!
....

MRS. ICHINOSE... DID THE MANAGER MENTION THIS TO YOU AT ALL?
NOT A WORD.

'SCUSE US!
BAM
WE'RE TH' MOVERS.
THUD THUD
Y'KNOW WHERE TH' MANAGER'S ROOM IS?
DOWN THE HALL AND LEFT.
THUD THUD

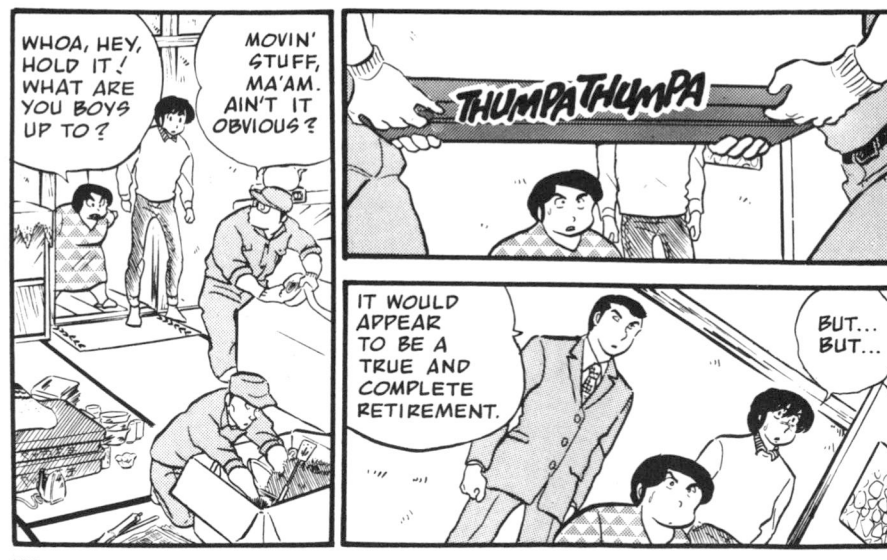

WHOA, HEY, HOLD IT! WHAT ARE YOU BOYS UP TO?
MOVIN' STUFF, MA'AM. AIN'T IT OBVIOUS?
THUMPATHUMPA
IT WOULD APPEAR TO BE A TRUE AND COMPLETE RETIREMENT.
BUT... BUT...

I...I CAN'T BELIEVE THIS!
SHE COULD HAVE AT LEAST SAID SOMETHING TO ME ABOUT IT!
ME...WHO TREATED HER JUST LIKE A SISTER...
PERHAPS YOU MEAN "DAUGHTER"...?
LIKE A SISTER!
AH, YES--OF COURSE.

WHY...?
WHY SO SUDDENLY...?

DAMN IT, I THOUGHT IT WAS STRANGE! HER STARTING TO FIX UP THE BUILDING LIKE THAT...
LIKE THEY SAY, "A DEPARTING BIRD LEAVES A CLEAN NEST."
BUT... SHE CAN'T JUST...
THUMP THUD

SLAM BRMMMM
JUST LEAVING... WITHOUT EVEN SAYING GOODBYE...
QUITE SO...BUT DON'T YOU RECALL...

THE OLD MAN WHO WAS THE PREVIOUS MANAGER--HE LEFT SUDDENLY AND MYSTERIOUSLY.
THEN SHE APPEARED... ALSO SUDDENLY AND MYSTERIOUSLY. HMM...
KYOKO AND THAT OLD MANAGER ARE *COMPLETELY* DIFFERENT!
WE GOT ALONG JUST LIKE *FAMILY*!
HOW COULD SHE DO THIS TO US?!
DAMN IT ALL... I NEED A GOOD STIFF DRINK!
YOU'RE COMING, TOO.
GRAB
WE HAVEN'T WALKED SO FAR IN AGES, HAVE WE, MR. SOICHIRO?
BOWF!
HELLO!
WHEW... I'M BEAT.
I NEED A NICE CUP OF TEA.
FLIP FLAP
OH, NO-- I MUST HAVE LEFT MY DOOR OPEN!
MANAGER

MR. YOTSUYA! WHAT ARE YOU DOING IN MY--
....
HWOOOOO
THUD
IT WAS ALL SO SUDDEN.
I WAS MERELY SORTING OUT MY FEELINGS.
WH... WHAT IN TH-?!
AFTER DEEP THOUGHT, I HAVE COME TO A CONCLUSION--

--SADLY, TRAGICALLY, WE HAVE NO RIGHT TO STOP YOU.
WHAT ARE YOU TALKING ABOUT ?

YOUR MOTHER CAME AND ANNOUNCED YOUR RETIREMENT, WITH DIGNITY AND GRACE.
SHE DID WHAT ?!
THEN SHE SUMMONED THE MOVERS...

MS. OTONASHI...
THUD THUD
I'M GOING TO MY PARENTS' HOUSE!

HERE! TAKE IT AND SHARE IT!
THUD THUD
.....
THUD THUD THUD THUD THUD
BAR
SO, THIS IS WHERE YOU HAVE ALL CONGREGATED.
THE TWO OF THEM ARE COMPLETELY PLASTERED.
NNNGRR! WHAT A FOOL I WASH *HIC* TO THINK SHE WAS SO SWEET AN' INNOSHENT!
WAAAH! KYOKO!
THE MANAGER SAID SHE WAS RETURNING TO HER PARENTS' RESIDENCE.
YOU SHAW HER?!
THIS WAS OFFERED AS A GOING-AWAY GIFT.
WHUZZAT?
HUH? CAKES?
DOESH SHE THINK SHE CAN BUY US OFF WITH SOME STINKIN' CAKESH?!
snff sob

LIKE SOME KINDA STINKIN' BRIBE
HEY, SAVE SOME FOR ME...
KYOKO... ⋛SNFF⋚
LOOK, MR. YOTSUYA--COULD YOU TAKE THEM BACK TO THE APARTMENT?
THEY'RE GOING TO SCARE OFF ALL MY OTHER CUSTOMERS.
VERY WELL.

AKEMI, YOU CAN KNOCK OFF EARLY AND GO BACK WITH THEM.
REALLY? THANKS, HON.
YOU MUST GO HOME NOW.
"GO HOME"..? ALREADY? ⋛HIC⋚ ARE YOU SOME KINDA NUT CASE?

GEE WHIZ, MOM--DON'T DRINK SO MUCH!
⋛snff⋚ ⋛sob⋚
SHUDDUP! AIN'T YOU SUPPOSTA BE IN BED?

AN' YOU! YA SNIVELIN' BRAT! WHAT KINDA MAN ARE YA, ANYWAY?!
B-BUT...THISH ISH SHO...SHO HORRIBLE!
AW, LEAVE THE KID ALONE.

I GOTTA ADMIT... IT WAS PRETTY COLD-HEARTED OF HER.
snff
SLAM
WHO'S THAT AT *THISH* HOUR?
IN ALL LIKELIHOOD, NOTHING MORE THAN THE WIND.
KCHAK
I CAN'T BELIEVE IT...
ITSH... IT'S *HER!!*
EH? WHAT ARE YOU ALL DOING HERE?
WHAT ARE *YOU* DOIN' HERE?! DID YOU FORGET SOMETHIN'?
WHAT ?

DIDN'T YOU GO BACK TO YOUR PARENTS' PLACE?
OF COURSE! TO TELL THEM TO RETURN MY THINGS!
I'M REALLY SORRY ABOUT ALL THIS TROUBLE.
IT WAS ALL MY MOTHER'S PLOT.
.....

I DON'T GET IT.
WAIT A SECOND...
...YOU MEAN YOU'RE NOT QUITTING?
OF COURSE NOT!
YAHOO! HOORAY!
ALL RIGHT!
GLOMP
GLOMP
YUSAKU! REALLY!
THANK YOU, GOD! THANKSH!
AW, HE'SH JUST DRUNK.
THISH CALLS FOR A CELEBRATION! HAVVA LIL' DRINKIE!
THANKS... MY THROAT IS SO DRY.
YOUR VOICE SOUNDS TOTALLY SHOT!
YES...I'M AFRAID I YELLED TOO MUCH.
KOFF

THANK YOU, EVERYONE...
...FOR CARING ABOUT ME.
AW, I ALWAYS KNEW SHE WOULDN'T LEAVE USH LIKE THAT.
A TOAST!
KLINK
HELLO?
CHING
RRIINNGG
SHH
.....
...BUT THE WAR ISN'T OVER YET!
DON'T YOU EVER QUIT, YOU OLD WITCH?!
YANK
OWW!
KYOKO? IT'S ME.
KOFF KOFF
YOU MAY HAVE WON THE BATTLE...

Part Nine

I'm Convinced

-SNIFF-
WHAT'S THE MATTER WITH YOU?
SHE WAS JUST SO CUTE...
ARE YOU GOING THROUGH THAT ALBUM AGAIN?
KYOKO'S FIRST DAY AT GRAMMAR SCHOOL.
BUT JUST LOOK AT THIS...
.....

SHE WAS SUCH A DARLING.
SUCH A SWEET, INNOCENT, THOUGHTFUL GIRL...
.....
PHOTOS...
MAYBE I CAN USE ONE...

DON'T YOU THINK THEY'RE A BIT STRANGE?
I MEAN, REALLY...
I THINK MY FAMILY IS DYSFUNCTIONAL.
NOW, KYOKO...
AREN'T YOU BEING A BIT HARSH?
AFTER ALL, THEY *ARE* YOUR PARENTS.
YES, BUT LOOK WHAT THEY DID-- HIRING MOVERS TO CLEAN OUT MY ROOM WHILE I WAS GONE!
WELL, TRUE ENOUGH.
DON'T YOU THINK THAT'S PRETTY WEIRD?
EVEN *CRIMINAL*?

I'M BEGINNING TO GET THE IDEA THAT YOU AND YOUR PARENTS DON'T GET ALONG WELL.
ISN'T THAT RATHER OBVIOUS ?
I WONDER WHY IT IS.
YOU'RE SUCH A SWEETHEART TO OTHER PEOPLE... SO WHY ARE YOU SO HARD ON YOUR PARENTS ?
BEING KIND TO THEM JUST ENCOURAGES THEM TO TAKE ADVANTAGE OF ME.
HERE'S A THOUGHT--DON'T YOU THINK IT MIGHT BE YOUR HARSHNESS THAT HAS TWISTED YOUR PARENTS' LOVE ?
WHOSE SIDE ARE YOU ON, ANYWAY ?
WELL, I'M A PARENT MYSELF, Y'KNOW.
CHILDREN SHOULD THANK GOD FOR THEIR PARENTS!
EACH AND EVERY DAY!
DOES MY KENTARO COMPLAIN ABOUT ME?!
WELL... UH...

SHE MAKES ME SO MAD!
NEW YORK

IT'S SPRING VACATION AND SHE WON'T TAKE ME ANYWHERE!
DIDN'T YOU HAVE THE SAME PROBLEM LAST SUMMER?

AND SHE DRINKS TOO MUCH! ALL THE TIME!
DON'T I HAVE THE RIGHT TO COMPLAIN SOMETIMES?
WELL, LISTEN TO THE LITTLE EXPERT!

WHO CARES ABOUT YOUR STUPID LITTLE PROBLEMS, ANYWAY?
I MEAN, THE MANAGER MIGHT BE STOLEN FROM US AT ANY MINUTE!

YOUR MOTHER'S TOUGH AS NAILS.
IF ANYONE CAN PROTECT KYOKO FROM HER PARENTS, SHE CAN!

HEY, YOU'RE THE ONE WITH A CRUSH ON THE MANAGER-- YOU PROTECT HER.
URK!

MAN, YOU'RE A WIMP!
IF YOU'RE GONNA COP THAT KIND OF ATTITUDE, SHE'S NEVER GONNA PAY ATTENTION TO YOU.
LISTEN, **BRAT**--
WELL, IT'S **TRUE**, ISN'T IT?!
HANGING AROUND ADULTS HAS GIVEN YOU A REAL MOUTH, KID!
BUT I REALLY **CAN'T** DO ANYTHING.
AS LONG AS OUR RELATIONSHIP IS JUST "MANAGER/TENANT"...
...WHAT RIGHT HAVE I TO ASK HER NOT TO GO?
WE'RE JUST STRANGERS...
GEEZ...
GEEZ...I WANNA GO ON A VACATION.

WHAT ARE YOU RUMMAGING AROUND FOR?
I HAVE A PLAN.

WHEN'S DINNER ?
IT'S ON THE TABLE.
I COME HOME EARLY FOR ONCE, AND--
OH, SHUT UP !
FLIP FLIP

AH, HA!
HERE IT IS!

WHIP

WHAT WERE YOU LOOKING FOR?
A TOOL TO BRING BACK KYOKO.
IT'S ALL THESE LITTLE TRICKS OF YOURS...
...THAT HAVE GIVEN KYOKO HER ATTITUDE, YOU KNOW.
ME?! YOU'RE THE ONE WHO STARTED IT ALL!

IF YOU'D SAID EVEN A SINGLE KIND WORD TO HER WHEN SOICHIRO DIED...
I DON'T WANT TO HEAR ABOUT IT!

KYOKO'S JUST BEING STUBBORN.
THE FIRST THING WE HAVE TO DO IS CUT HER TIES TO THE OTONASHI FAMILY.
THAT'S WHAT'S KEEPING HER FROM GETTING REMARRIED.
ANOTHER BOWL?
YES, PLEASE.

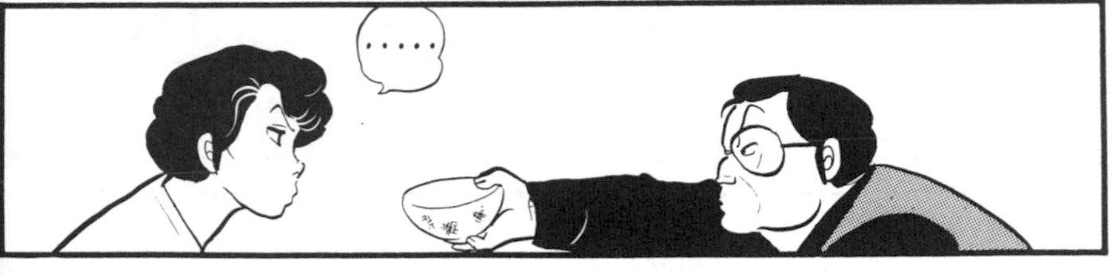
.....

YOU'VE CERTAINLY GOT A GOOD APPETITE!
JUST HOW INSENSITIVE ARE YOU?!
YOU SHOULD BE WORRIED SICK ABOUT YOUR DAUGHTER! WHY, I NEVER...
NAG NAG NAG

SUNDAY
ARE YOU OKAY, MOM?
WHAT DO YOU MEAN, AM I OKAY?
SHOPPING
COFFEE
I DUNNO... IT'S JUST THAT YOU HARDLY EVER TAKE ME TO THE MOVIES.
WELL, A MOTHER NEEDS TO SPEND SOME QUALITY TIME WITH HER SON.
ARE YOU HAVING FUN?
Mistral
SENTO
YEAH!

CLOCK HILL STATION

CLACK CLACK CLACK

LET'S SEE... "BUSYBODY, EXTREMELY INQUISITIVE..."

"...EASILY FLATTERED, EASILY MANIPULATED."

MRS. ICHINOSE... IF I CAN GET HER WITHIN MY GRASP...

FWAP

BUT HOW CAN I ARRANGE TO MEET HER?
IF I GO TO MAISON IKKOKU, KYOKO MIGHT SEE ME...
SHOPPI
ALL
Book
Ginseng Tea
MY, ISN'T *THIS* A COINCIDENCE...
SAY... AREN'T YOU--
THE GODS THEMSELVES MUST HAVE BROUGHT US TOGETHER.
?
I DESPERATELY NEEDED TO SPEAK WITH YOU TODAY, MRS. ICHINOSE.
OH, YEAH?
WHY WOULD YOU WANT TO SPEAK WITH *ME*?
WELL... YOU SEE...
SUN MA

Y-YOU'RE THE ONLY PERSON I CAN TURN TO...

HMM...
.....

LOOK, LET'S NOT STAND HERE IN THE STREET.
Y-YOU MEAN...

...YOU'LL LISTEN TO WHAT I HAVE TO SAY?
YEAH.
AW, MOM!
WHAT ABOUT THE MOVIE ?!
SORRY, BUT THIS SOUNDS MORE INTERESTING THAN A MOVIE.
Today's Special

SWALLOWED HOOK, LINE, AND SINKER.
OH, DON'T COMPLAIN. I'LL BUY YOU SOMETHING YUMMY TO EAT INSTEAD.
YOU KEEP TREATING ME LIKE THIS AND I'M GONNA JOIN A GANG!
NO KIDDING? MRS. ICHINOSE TOOK KENTARO TO A MOVIE?

DOESN'T SOUND LIKE HER. I WONDER WHY...
SEEING KYOKO'S PROBLEMS WITH HER PARENTS GOT HER WORRIED, PROBABLY.
GEEZ, NICE TALK, AKEMI!
AW, SHE DOESN'T MIND, 'CAUSE IT'S TRUE, RIGHT?
WELL...
RRIINNGG
!!
WHAT'S THE PROB? ANSWER IT ALREADY!
RRIINNGG
BUT WHAT IF IT'S MY MOTHER...?
RRIINNGG
OH, BROTHER.
SHOULD I ANSWER IT?
RRIINNGG
IF IT'S MY MOTHER, I'M NOT HERE!
YEAH, YEAH.
CHING.
HELLO...
OTONASHI RESIDENCE.
YES...
...SHE'S HERE.

IT'S A MAN.
REALLY?
A... A MAN? WHO IS IT?
HELLO?
HEY, I CAN'T KEEP TRACK OF ALL HER LITTLE LOVE AFFAIRS.
FATHER?!
"LOVE AFFAIRS," HUH?!
SURE-- FATHERS LOVE THEIR DAUGHTERS, DON'T THEY?
IS YOUR MOTHER THERE NOW?
WHAT?
NO, SHE'S NOT.
WHY DO YOU ASK?
WELL, IT'S JUST THAT...
...I REALLY WANT TO TALK WITH YOU ALONE.
THINGS ALWAYS GET MIXED UP WHEN YOUR MOTHER IS THERE.
UM...

SO IS IT ALL RIGHT IF I COME OVER NOW?
YES. SURE. SEE YOU.

SO WHAT'S UP ?
CHAK
MY DAD'S COMING OVER.
OH, YEAH ?!
HE...HE COULD BE COMING TO TAKE HER AWAY!
IF THAT OLD FART TRIES TO DRAG HER BACK BY FORCE, I'LL...
...I'LL STOP HIM BY FORCE!
I'VE GOT TO DO SOMETHING.
K-KYOKO, YOUR FATHER IS HERE!
HE'S WHAT ?!

WELL, THAT WAS QUICK, DAD!
I CALLED FROM THE PAY PHONE JUST DOWN THE BLOCK.
C'MON, KID--WE BETTER SCOOT.
YEAH, SURE.
WE'VE BEEN SO STUBBORN WITH EACH OTHER OVER THE YEARS...
...NOW SHE JUST WON'T LISTEN TO ANYTHING I SAY.
CHINESE FOOD
MAMA-SAN
MAMA-SAN
PARDON ME FOR INTRUDING, BUT I'VE HEARD ABOUT YOU FROM YOUR NEIGHBORS.
YOU ASKED THEM ABOUT ME?
THEY TOLD ME YOU'VE BEEN TAKING GOOD CARE OF MY KYOKO.
YEAH, SURE... IT'S LIKE HAVING A YOUNGER SISTER.
BLUP BLUP
THEN I'M SURE SHE'LL LISTEN TO SENSE IF SHE HEARS IT FROM YOU, MRS. ICHINOSE!
PLEASE TELL HER TO COME BACK HOME!
GRAB

KLIK
THE TRUTH IS THAT HER FATHER...
...HAS A WEAK CONSTITUTION, AND IS ALWAYS IN AND OUT OF THE HOSPITAL.
Get Well Soon
OH, I'M SO SORRY.
THIS IS THE FIRST I'VE HEARD OF IT.
THAT AWFUL CHILD WON'T EVEN COME TO SEE HIM IN THE HOSPITAL.
HEY, YUSAKU TOLD ME HE SAW THE MANAGER'S DAD OUTSIDE THE APARTMENT ONCE.
GOOD HEAVENS !
HE MUST HAVE SNUCK OUT OF THE HOSPITAL...
...JUST TO SEE HIS ONLY DAUGHTER!
I HAVE TO GET MY DAUGHTER BACK.
NO MATTER WHAT CRAZY STEPS I MAY HAVE TO TAKE...
I SEE.
WELL, NO WONDER THEY HAD TO RESORT TO SENDING MOVERS TO TAKE HER STUFF AWAY!
I'M CONVINCED.
I'LL TALK SOME SENSE INTO THAT GIRL!
TH-THANK YOU !!
GRAB

SO I GUESS...
...I WAS WRONG, TOO.
BUT I STILL WANT YOU TO STOP BEING SO STUBBORN AND MOVE BACK HOME.
LOOK, DADDY...
THE FACT THAT YOU OPPOSED MY MARRIAGE...
...AND THAT YOU OFFERED ME NO SUPPORT WHEN SOICHIRO DIED...

...AND THAT YOU'VE NEVER COME TO HIS GRAVE WITH ME ON THE ANNIVERSARY OF HIS DEATH...
...AND, WELL, THE LIST GOES ON AND ON.
QUIVER
BUT I'VE FORGOTTEN ABOUT ALL THAT.
YOU... YOU HAVE?
PANT PANT PANT
I'M NOT A CHILD ANYMORE, FATHER.
I'LL DECIDE FOR MYSELF WHAT'S BEST FOR ME.
RRG...
THIS IS THE THANKS I GET FOR APOLOGIZING SO NICELY...
VOOM
YOU'RE GOING ?
TO THE BATHROOM.
KREEK

SIGHH...
HE STILL DOESN'T GET IT.
THUD THUD THUD
GOOD! YOU'RE HERE!
WHAM
YOU KNOW, YOU REALLY SHOULD GO BACK HOME!
WHA-?!
YOU SHOULD THINK ABOUT HOW YOUR FATHER FEELS, ONCE IN A WHILE!
NAG NAG NAG NAG
NAG NAG
WHERE DID THIS COME FROM?!
REMEMBER, YOUR PARENTS WON'T ALWAYS BE THERE FOR YOU...
NAG NAG NAG NAG
AND WITH YOUR FATHER, IT MIGHT--
I SECOND THAT OPINION!
WHO ARE YOU?
AH, EXCUSE ME-- IT'S A PLEASURE TO MEET YOU.

I'M KYOKO'S FATHER.
EH ?
YES.
IS HE REALLY ?
WELL, YOU CERTAINLY LOOK HEALTHY.
I AM INDEED, THANK YOU.
HUH...THAT'S STRANGE. HE DOESN'T LOOK ANYTHING LIKE THAT PICTURE...
WHAT PICTURE ?
YOUR MOTHER SHOWED IT TO ME TODAY.
HIM IN THE HOSPITAL, LOOKING LIKE THIS.
YOU MET WITH MY MOTHER ?!
SHE TRICKED YOU !!
THAT PICTURE IS FROM MORE THAN FIVE YEARS AGO!!
I'M CONVINCED.
NOW DO YOU UNDERSTAND? MY MOTHER IS INSANE!
ARE YOU CRAZY ?!
THAT PLAN HAD ENOUGH HOLES IN IT TO DRAIN RAMEN WITH!
YOU! WHY DID YOU GO SNEAKING OVER THERE WITHOUT TELLING ME?!
I ALMOST HAD ICHINOSE ON OUR SIDE!

Part Ten

I'll Never Give Up!

HMM ?
MY, MY... GOING OUT ?
WHAT'S UP ?
SOMETHING'S GOING ON DOWN AT THE END OF THE HALLWAY.
YOU MEAN BY KYOKO'S ROOM ?
THAP THAP THAP
YEAH... LOOKS GRIM.
I'M GLAD TO SEE YOU LOOKING SO WELL.
THANK YOU...AND MY BACK FEELS BETTER, TOO.
THAT'S GRAMPA OTONASHI.
AND KYOKO'S PARENTS...

KYOKO, WE'LL BE WAITING OUTSIDE.
ALL RIGHT!
...ETTE PAPER
LET ME HELP YOU, FATHER OTONASHI.
THANK YOU, MY DEAR.
I DON'T LIKE THE LOOK OF THIS ONE BIT.
ME, EITHER!
SAY... ISN'T TODAY...?
THAP
THAP
THAP

YOU GOING OUT TOO, KYOKO ?
YES.

YOU'RE... YOU'RE VISITING SOICHIRO'S GRAVE, AREN'T YOU ?
YES.
AH, I SEE.
IN THAT CASE THERE'S NOTHING ODD ABOUT BOTH FAMILIES BEING TOGETHER.
OH, YES THERE IS.

EVERY YEAR MY PARENTS MAKE UP SOME LAME EXCUSE NOT TO GO.
I'LL BE BACK BY EVENING.
YOU DON'T FIGURE THEY'LL HAVE A FIGHT IN FRONT OF THE GRAVE, DO YOU ?
WELL...

GRAMPA OTONASHI SURE IS A EASYGOING GUY...
HE FORGAVE KYOKO'S PARENTS JUST LIKE *THAT*.
DAMN !
I WISH I HADN'T MADE THIS DATE.
NOT THAT I COULD TAG ALONG WITH THEM, ANYWAY.
RATS !
YOW!
DID I SCARE YOU ?!
YES !
GREAT, YOU PUT ON A TIE!
YOU LOOK SO *NICE!*
YOU TOLD ME TO WEAR IT!

WHERE ARE WE GOING ?
JUST FOLLOW ME AND YOU'LL FIND OUT!
WHAT'S WITH THE MELON ?

HEE, HEE !
YOU LOOK GREAT...
REALLY ?
I'M SO PROUD !

HERE WE ARE.
...?

NANAO

YOUR...
IT'S MY HOUSE.

COME ON IN !
HEY, HEY, WAIT A SEC! YOU NEVER SAID...

I MEAN, I'M NOT READY...
AW, DON'T BE SHY !

HE SEEMS LIKE A NICE YOUNG MAN.

WHAT DID YOU EXPECT, DADDY ?

I FEEL LIKE A DISSECTION SPECIMEN.

AND IT WAS SO THOUGHTFUL OF YOU TO BRING THIS MELON.

YUSAKU'S SO CONSIDERATE, ISN'T HE ?

HEY SIS, YOU TWO GUYS KISSED YET ?

WELLLLLL...

WHAT'S WRONG WITH "NO"?!

AWW, C'MON. HOW FAR'D YA GET WITH SIS ALREADY?
NOWHERE, THANK YOU!
YOSUKE!
QUIT BEING SUCH A BRAT!
HE MIGHT BE YOUR BROTHER-IN-LAW SOME DAY!
...!
I HAVEN'T EVEN KISSED HER YET...
...AND SHE'S ALREADY TALKING ABOUT "BROTHER-IN-LAW"!!
NOW, YUSAKU DEAR, KOZUE'S JUST A CHILD.
I HOPE YOUR INTENTIONS TOWARD MY DAUGHTER ARE HONORABLE.
WELL, I...UH...
THAT'S ENOUGH OF THAT!
C'MON, LET ME SHOW YOU MY ROOM!
.....

I'M SURE SOICHIRO IS VERY PLEASED...

...TO HAVE YOU OFFER UP INCENSE THIS WAY.

OH, IT'S NOTHING.

WE WOULD HAVE COME LAST YEAR TOO, IF MY HUSBAND HADN'T BEEN ILL.

HMPH... YOU MADE THAT UP!

WELL, THAT COULDN'T BE HELPED.

SOICHIRO, I'M SORRY I HAVEN'T BEEN HERE FOR SO LONG.

YOU MUST HAVE BEEN LONELY.

PLEASE DON'T WORRY ABOUT ME.
I'M ENJOYING LIVING AND WORKING AT MAISON IKKOKU.

TIME GOES BY SO QUICKLY.
IT'S ALREADY BEEN TWO YEARS SINCE HE PASSED AWAY.
YES...
TWO YEARS HAVE FLOWN BY.
YES, TWO WHOLE YEARS.
BUT I'M SURE YOU STILL CAN'T FORGET YOUR SON, FATHER OTONASHI.
DON'T YOU WORRY ABOUT ME...HOW ABOUT POOR KYOKO?
YOU CAN'T STAY LIKE THIS FOREVER, KYOKO...MARRIED TO MY SON'S MEMORY.
NOW, FATHER...
NO, I'VE GIVEN THIS A LOT OF THOUGHT.
IT'S NOT GOOD FOR YOU TO STAY IN MOURNING.
NOT GOOD AT ALL.
YOU'RE STILL YOUNG, KYOKO--
IT'S ABOUT TIME YOU WITHDREW FROM THE OTONASHI FAMILY REGISTER AND STARTED A NEW LIFE.
WHY?! HOW...?!

DID YOU PUT THAT IDEA INTO HIS HEAD ?
I WAS PLANNING TO, BUT...
WHY ARE YOU SAYING THIS ?
WHAT DO YOU MEAN, "START A NEW LIFE"...?
ARE YOU TELLING ME TO FORGET SOICHIRO?
YOU KNOW, KYOKO...
...IN THE OLD DAYS, WHEN A HUSBAND DIED...
...THEY WOULD WRITE THE NAME OF HIS WIDOW ON THE HEADSTONE, TOO...IN RED INK.
TO BE A WIDOW...
...MEANT SIMPLY TO BE A WIFE WHO WASN'T DEAD YET.
BUT THAT'S NOT THE WAY IT IS NOW, IS IT?
IT'S NOT THAT YOU'RE NOT DEAD YET...
IT'S THAT YOU'RE ALIVE.

ISN'T THAT A LOVELY THOUGHT, MOTHER?
IT'S A VERY *WELCOME* THOUGHT.
KYOKO, YOU HAVE TO GET OVER SOICHIRO.
SNIFFLE

IS...IS IT A PROBLEM FOR ME TO STAY A PART OF YOUR FAMILY?
OF COURSE NOT, KYOKO!
ON THE CONTRARY, YOU'RE VERY DEAR TO OUR HEARTS.

WE'RE THANKFUL THAT YOU LOVED OUR SON SO DEEPLY.
BUT YOUR LIFE...
PLEASE LET ME BE SELFISH A LITTLE WHILE LONGER!
KYOKO!
DON'T YOU APPRECIATE THAT FATHER OTONASHI IS ONLY CONCERNED FOR YOU AND YOUR FUTURE?

I DO.
I UNDERSTAND WHAT HE'S SAYING... ON AN INTELLECTUAL LEVEL.

KYOKO...
WHAT DO YOU INTEND TO DO?
I...I DON'T KNOW YET.
BUT UNTIL I **DO** DECIDE WHAT TO DO...
...I WANT TO KEEP MY HUSBAND'S NAME.
THAT'S EASY FOR YOU TO SAY, BUT WHILE YOU'RE DECIDING, TIME'S GOING BY! PRETTY SOON YOU'LL BE AN OLD MAID!
.....
HAVEN'T YOU MET A MAN YOU LIKE YET?
WELL, KYOKO?
THIS IS **NOT** THE PLACE TO DISCUSS THIS!
.....

I THINK MOM AND DAD LIKE YOU, YUSAKU! ISN'T THAT GREAT?
THAT'S JUST FINE, BUT...
THIS KIND OF FORMAL SCENE... IT'S LIKE... I DUNNO... IT'S LIKE...
LIKE WHAT?
IT'S IMPORTANT TO GET TO KNOW THE OTHER PERSON'S PARENTS, ISN'T IT?
.....

AFTER ALL, A MARRIAGE IS A MARRIAGE OF TWO FAMILIES...
MUH-MUH-MUH-MARRIAGE?!

I THINK EVERYTHING GOES MORE SMOOTHLY IF YOU INCLUDE THE PARENTS, TOO.
YEAH, THAT'S TRUE...

BUT CAN I GET ALONG WITH THOSE PARENTS...?

DO YOU THINK YOU CAN GET ALONG WITH THEM?
I'M NOT SO SURE...
HUH?
NOTHING, NOTHING. JUST THINKING OUT LOUD.
YOU KNOW, KOZUE...
...YOU'VE GOT THINGS BACKWARD, HERE.
USUALLY YOU DO THIS SORT OF THING AFTER YOU'VE BEGUN TO HAVE A SERIOUS RELATIONSHIP.
THAT'S TRUE... WE'VE HAD KIND OF A PLATONIC RELATIONSHIP SO FAR.
WHY HAVEN'T YOU TRIED ANYTHING?
WELL?
.....

WHRRR WHRRR WHRRR WHRRR (The GEARS TURN)
SHOULD I DO IT, OR SHOULDN'T I ?
IT'S JUST A KISS...
NO, NO... WAIT A MINUTE...
AHA! CAUGHT IN THE ACT!!
BAM
NOW LET'S SEE YOU PROVE YOUR HONORABLE INTENTIONS--
LET'S ALL GO DOWN TO CITY HALL TO REGISTER YOUR MARRIAGE.
OUR SWEET KOZUE IS JUST A CHILD, YOU SEE.
Y-YOU CAN'T BE--
B-BUT IT WAS JUST A KISS...
"JUST"... ?!
ARE YOU SAYING YOU KISSED OUR DAUGHTER FOR CHEAP THRILLS?!
NO! WAIT! STOP! HELP! MAMA!
"MAMA"...?

DID YOU HEAR THAT, DEAR?
YUSAKU CALLED ME "MAMA"!
SO YOU'VE FINALLY COME TO YOUR SENSES, EH, MY BOY?
WELL, I DON'T HOLD A GRUDGE!
GO AHEAD... CALL HIM "PAPA"!
WHRRR WHRRR KRACH!
BRRR...R...
HEY! SOMEBODY'S LOOKING IN THE WINDOW!
WHAT?!
MUST BE MY ROTTEN LITTLE BROTHER...
NOBODY'S HERE...
NO KIDDING? MUST HAVE BEEN A TRICK OF THE LIGHT.
WE'RE ON THE SECOND FLOOR, TOO.

AW, YUSAKU, PLEEEASE STAY A WHILE LONGER!
YES, DEAR... WHY DON'T YOU STAY AND HAVE DINNER WITH US?
I'M SORRY... I HAVE SOME STUFF I'VE GOT TO DO.
WELL, DON'T BE A STRANGER, NOW!
YES, MA'AM!
NANAO
WHEW... WHAT A NIGHTMARE!
3:30...
"I'LL BE BACK BY EVENING..."
CLACK
CLACK
WITH THAT BUNCH, THE TRIP HAS TO HAVE ENDED IN DISASTER!
POOR KYOKO...
CLOCK HILL STATION
NOODLES
BEST NOODLES IN TOWN!

PLEASE STAND CLEAR OF THE EDGE...
I BET SHE COMES BACK DEPRESSED.
BRRIINNGG
THERE'S NOT MUCH I CAN DO...
...EXCEPT CONSOLE HER A BIT.
BUT STILL, I--

YOU'RE **HOPELESS**! EVEN MR. OTONASHI AGREES WITH ME!
THIS WOULD BE THE PERFECT TIME!
WOULD YOU TWO JUST **SHUT UP**! I'M TIRED OF HEARING THE SAME THING OVER AND OVER AGAIN!!
STOMP STOMP
NOODLES
!
THE BEST

WE WOULDN'T HAVE TO REPEAT OURSELVES, IF YOU'D JUST **LISTEN** FOR ONCE!
?!
STOMP STOMP
DON'T FOLLOW ME!
NAG NAG NAG NAG
YOU COULD AT **LEAST** GO BACK TO YOUR MAIDEN NAME!!
DROP IT!

UM...
HOW LONG DO YOU INTEND TO MILK THE "POOR OLD WIDOW" ACT?!
STOMP STOMP
WOULD YOU MIND KEEPING YOUR VOICE DOWN?! PEOPLE ARE STARING !!

UM... KYOKO...
NAG NAG NAG NAG
SHUT UP SHUT UP SHUT UP!

I...I COULD NEVER CUT IT IN THAT FAMILY.
I GIVE UP...
YOU THINK I'M GIVING UP? I'VE ONLY JUST BEGUN TO FIGHT!
I'LL NEVER GIVE UP !!
STOMP STOMP!

Part Eleven

Mixed (Up) Doubles

AHHH...
SKREEK.
OUTTA THE WAY, SON!
WHY ARE YOU WASHING THE FLOOR UP HERE?
ISN'T IT OBVIOUS? I'M HELPING OUT THE MANAGER.
WE'RE PLAYING TENNIS TODAY.
TENNIS?!
YES, TENNIS. WHAT'S WITH THE FACE?
YOU KNOW KYOKO'S HAVING PROBLEMS WITH HER PARENTS...
...TELLING HER TO QUIT HER JOB AS MANAGER HERE...
...AND TO SIGN HERSELF OUT OF THE OTONASHI FAMILY REGISTER.

SO THIS WILL HELP HER FORGET HER PROBLEMS.
YEAH, BUT YOU DON'T HAVE TO PLAY *TENNIS*.
WELL, THEN, DO ***YOU*** HAVE ANY BRIGHT IDEAS TO MAKE HER FEEL BETTER?
GARGLE GARGLE
......

BESIDES, THAT HUNKY MITAKA'S GOING TO BE THERE, TOO.
GULK.
KYOKO'S ***THRILLED*** ABOUT IT.
AHUK AHUK
THANKS A LOT, MRS. ICHINOSE.
I'VE GOT THE FIRST FLOOR ALL DONE.
THEN WE'RE OFF.

THIS IS GREAT! IT'S BEEN ***SO*** LONG SINCE WE PLAYED!
SEE WHAT I MEAN? ***THRILLED.***
HMPH! ASK ME IF I CARE!
TUMP TUMP TUMP

KA-
POK
KPOK
HEH...NOTHING LIKE A LITTLE EXERCISE TO CHEER YOU UP, IS THERE?

YOU KNOW...KYOKO HASN'T BEEN COMING TO THE CLASS TOO OFTEN LATELY, HAS SHE?
SOME KINDA PROBLEM?
YEAH, WELL, SORT OF.
SHE'S HAVING SOME COMPLICATED FAMILY PROBLEMS...
HEY!!
COLLECTIONS
WHAT?
WHY DON'T YOU KEEP YOUR GOSSIP TO YOURSELF?
WHY? IT'S NOT LIKE THIS IS SOME SORT OF TERRIBLE "DARK SECRET."
WELL, MAYBE NOT, BUT KYOKO IS A VERY SENSITIVE GIRL, YOU KNOW.
SOUNDS JUICY, EH?
THE WAY THEY TALK, YEAH!
LOOK, SHE'S FINALLY FORGET-TING HER PROBLEMS.
WE SHOULD LET IT REST, OKAY?
COLLECTIONS
WHAT PROBLEMS? WHO?

NONE OF YOUR DAMN BUSINESS, MITAKA !
IF IT'S ABOUT KYOKO, THEN IT IS MY BUSINESS, KID!
IT SEEMS SOME HEAVY BURDEN IS WEIGHING ON HER SOUL RIGHT NOW...
KPOK
YOU CAN TELL ?
INDEED...SUBTLE DISTURBANCES IN HER RETURNS SPEAK OF CONFUSION IN HER HEART.
KPOK
WOW...
YOU REALLY ARE A PRO, AREN'T YOU?
WELL... AHEM.
YOU'RE PULLING OUR LEG, RIGHT?
YOU CAN TELL ?
SHKK

LOOK, PLEASE TELL ME WHAT'S BOTHERING HER.
IF THERE'S ANYTHING AT ALL I CAN DO-- ANYTHING-- I'LL DO IT.
GEE...ALMOST SOUNDS LIKE HE'S MAKING A PASS AT ME, HUH?
NOT A CHANCE, DEARIE.
WHAT'S UP, EVERYBODY?
SO...YOU FEELING BETTER AFTER WORKING UP A SWEAT?
YOU BET!
SHKK
KYOKO...
YES?
I WANT TO CARRY HALF YOUR BURDEN...
EH...?
SHRKK
HEY, YOU!!
SHK!K

HAVEN'T YOU GOT ANYTHING BETTER TO DO, YUSAKU?

YEAH...IT'S SPRING BREAK--WHY DON'T YOU GO TO THE BEACH OR SOMETHING?

AREN'T YOU A UNIVERSITY STUDENT ?

MAKE THAT "A WRETCHED, PENNILESS, UNIVERSITY STUDENT."

WHAT ON EARTH HAVE YOU BEEN TALKING ABOUT ?

AW, NOTHIN', NOTHIN' AT ALL.!

STILL, HE'S GOT A POINT.

HOW LONG DO YOU INTEND TO STAND THERE CLUTCHING AT THE FENCE?

WHY SHOULDN'T I?!

'CAUSE IT'S **PATHETIC,** AT YOUR AGE!

NAG NAG

KIND OF **WEIRD,** IF YOU ASK ME!

NAG NAG

EEP!

NAG NAG

HEY, WHY DON'T YOU PLAY SOME TENNIS, TOO?
COULD I?
GEEZ, THAT WOULD BE GREAT!
I WAS GETTING KINDA TIRED OF JUST STARING THROUGH THE FENCE, ANYWAY.
HOLD ON A SECOND!

THIS IS A CLASS FOR HOUSEWIVES *ONLY*.
OH, DON'T BE SO PICKY, COACH!
BESIDES, IF YOU DON'T LET YOUNG BOYS LIKE HIM WORK OFF SOME OF THAT EXCESS ENERGY, THEY END UP COM-MITTING AWFUL SEX CRIMES.
WHAT KINDA SICK TALK IS THAT?!

OH, VERY WELL. GUESS I CAN GIVE YOU A FEW POINTERS.
HUH?
I'M GOING TO PLAY AGAINST *YOU*?!
WHOM DID YOU EXPECT TO PLAY WITH?
AWW...BUT YOU'RE SURE TO WIN, COACH!
YEAH, IT'S NO FUN WATCHING A MATCH THAT'S A SURE THING!
GEEZ... SUGAR-COAT IT, WHY DON'T YA?

WELL THEN, HOW ABOUT A GAME OF MIXED DOUBLES ?
OH, YEAH.
SURE! DEPENDING ON THE MIX, IT MIGHT BE WORTH WATCHING.
KYOKO, YOU CAN BE MY PARTNER...
UH...YOU WANT ME TO PLAY, TOO?
HEY, IN ORDER TO MAKE THINGS FAIR, SHE SHOULD BE WITH ME!!
WHAT DO YOU THINK ?
WELL, THE COACH REALLY NEEDS TO BE GIVEN SOME SORT OF HANDICAP.
SO, KYOKO... IF YOU DON'T MIND...?
SURE !
....
JUST CALL ME "MRS. HANDICAP."
UM...YOU DO MORE OR LESS KNOW THE RULES, RIGHT?
YEAH, WELL, PRETTY MUCH.

OF COURSE YOU KNOW THE RULES, RIGHT, MRS. ICHINOSE?
NOT AT ALL.
....
"NOT AT ALL"...?
NOT IN THE SLIGHTEST.
AND JUST HOW LONG HAVE YOU BEEN COMING TO THIS TENNIS CLASS ?!
HEY, HAVE YOU EVER SEEN ME PRACTICING AT ALL?
WELL, NO...
SEE ?
LOOK, IT DOESN'T MATTER WHO WINS OR LOSES IN THIS CASE.
IT'S JUST TO HELP KYOKO CHEER UP, RIGHT?
HMM...
ALL RIGHT, LET'S WORK UP A GOOD SWEAT!
RIGHT !

WHSSH
KA-PO
WHUPS !
KPOK

SPORT
WHAT A SHOT...
GUESS WE LOST THAT ONE, EH?
BWAHAHA
.....
FIFTEEN-LOVE!
WHA-?
15
0

B...BUT WHY? I RETURNED IT!
ER... YUSAKU...
I HAVE TO RETURN THE FIRST SERVE.
YOU? REALLY?
THAT'S FUNNY... WHY IS THAT?
IT'S JUST THE RULES, THAT'S ALL.
HEY, HE DOESN'T KNOW THE RULES EITHER!
MAYBE WE CAN WIN AFTER ALL!
UM... I'M SORRY.
AW, THAT'S OKAY... I'LL COVER FOR YOU.
KA-... POKK
ACTUALLY, YOU DON'T HAVE TO DO ANYTHING, MRS. ICHINOSE.
REALLY? GREAT!
POK

SINCE I HAVEN'T GOT ANYTHING TO DO, I'LL TALK TO YOU.
NO TALKING DURING THE MATCH, PLEASE !!
KPOK
CAN I HIT THIS --
GOT IT!
KPOK
...SO, ANYWAY, SHE MAY BE FORCED TO QUIT AS MANAGER.
WHAT WAS THAT ?
KPOK
HOW ABOUT THIS ONE?
GO FOR IT !
KPOK!
GOOD ONE!
YEAH, HER PARENTS WANT HER TO REMARRY.
EH ?!
POK
HEY ?!

ALL RIGHT!
I ALWAYS KNEW YOU HAD IT IN YOU, YUSAKU!
COLLECTION
CLAP CLAP
REMARRY? YOU MEAN THERE'S ALREADY SOMEONE?
WHOOPS... HERE COMES THE SERVE.
HEY, YOU HEAR THAT?
WOW!
WELL, THEY DON'T SEEM TO HAVE ANYONE IN MIND, BUT...
NO...NO KIDDING?
KPOK
MY GOODNESS!
WISH THEY'D SPEAK UP!
FIRST THEY WANT HER TO GO BACK TO HER MAIDEN NAME... THEN THEY WANT HER TO CUT HER TIES TO THE OTONASHI FAMILY.
NATTER NATTER
HMM...
WELL, WELL...
KPOK
KAPOK

KYOKO, MOVE FORWARD !
YUSAKU, YOU STEP BACK!
HM ?
HEY !
KPOK
ECTIONS

NOW I UNDERSTAND WHAT'S GOING ON...
POK
WHAT ?
THEY MAY BE GOING ABOUT IT THE WRONG WAY, BUT I CAN CERTAINLY UNDERSTAND HOW YOUR PARENTS FEEL.
POK

YOU WHAT ?!
POK
YOU SHOULD QUIT YOUR JOB AS APARTMENT MANAGER AND MAKE A FULL BREAK WITH THE PAST.

I WANT TO PAIR WITH YOU... FOR LIFE.

POK
HEY! WHAT ARE YOU SAYING ?!
YOU HEARD ME.
GEE... GUESS I SHOULDN'T HAVE BROUGHT THIS UP NOW, EH?
MY, MY!
MAYBE NOT, HMM?
LOUNGE
SALE
YOU'RE A REAL BLABBER-MOUTH, AREN'T YOU?
AH, BUT I PICK MY AUDIENCE WITH CARE, DON'T I?
THIS ISN'T DOING A THING TO HELP KYOKO WITH HER WORRIES, Y'KNOW!
HEY, AS IF JUST FORGETTING IT WOULD DO ANY GOOD!
COLLECTIONS
THAT'S RIGHT! SHE SHOULD TAKE THIS OPPORTUNITY TO THINK SERIOUSLY ABOUT REMARRYING!
OH, YEAH?! REMARRY WITH WHO?!

LOOK...NOBODY'S TAKING KYOKO'S FEELINGS INTO CONSIDERATION AT ALL, HERE!
.....
COLLECTIONS
DO SPORTS VITA
SHE'S NOT DOING THIS JUST TO ANNOY HER PARENTS, YOU KNOW!
KYOKO IS... SHE'S...
COFFEE
S-SHE'S... S-STILL IN L-L-LOVE WITH HER... HER LATE HUSBAND...
DAMN! THAT WAS HARD TO SAY!
SO...SO THERE'S NO POINT IN EVERYONE TRYING TO TELL HER WHAT TO DO, OKAY?
MUZUNO
COFFEE
YUSAKU...

WELL, YUSAKU MAY HAVE GOTTEN THE BEST OF ME TODAY...
...BUT I WAS SERIOUS WHEN I SAID I WANTED TO PAIR WITH YOU PERMANENTLY.
OH, COACH...
I'M SO SORRY, BUT IT WOULDN'T BE RIGHT.
NOT RIGHT ?!
I'M FLATTERED, BUT BEFORE I CAN PAIR WITH YOU PERMANENTLY...
...I REALLY HAVE TO WORK ON MY SERVE!
DOING
WHY DIDN'T I JUST SAY IT?! "MARRIAGE"! "MARRIAGE"! "MARRIAGE"!
KEEP OFF
YUSAKU, THANKS FOR WHAT YOU SAID.
YOU'RE THE ONLY ONE WHO REALLY UNDERSTANDS HOW I FEEL.
AW, GEE... HEH.
NOW IF ONLY YOU UNDER-STOOD HOW I FEEL.
COLLECTIONS

Part Twelve

Wait Three Years

HUH? YEAH, SURE, I'M EATING OKAY.
UM, I'M KINDA IN A HURRY, GRAN!
SURE, SURE, I'M FINE. IS MOM--
HI, GRANNY? IS MOM AROUND?
C'MON, GRANNY! I GOTTA GET TO SCHOOL!
YES, YES, I'M WASHING BEHIND MY EARS!
AND I'M CLEANING UNDER MY FINGERNAILS!
COACH MITAKA'S HERE TO PICK YOU UP!
HEY, KYOKO!
COMING!
WOOF WURF WUFF
WHAT IS IT WITH OLD PEOPLE, ANYWAY?
GEEZ LOUISE!
HONK HONK
WHAT'S THAT RACKET...?
HONK HONK

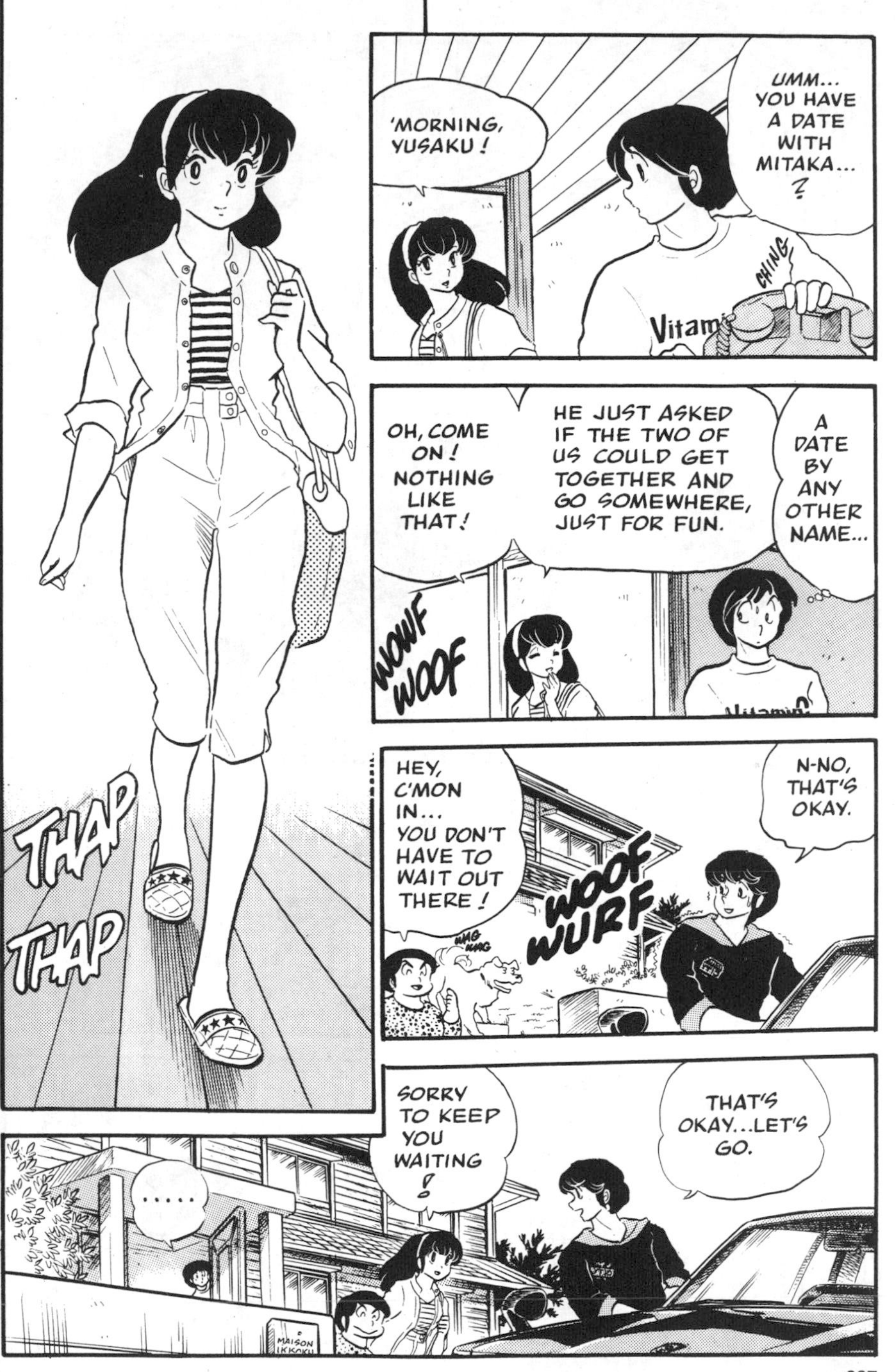
UMM... YOU HAVE A DATE WITH MITAKA...?
'MORNING, YUSAKU!
CHING
THAP THAP
A DATE BY ANY OTHER NAME...
HE JUST ASKED IF THE TWO OF US COULD GET TOGETHER AND GO SOMEWHERE, JUST FOR FUN.
OH, COME ON! NOTHING LIKE THAT!
WOWF WOOF
N-NO, THAT'S OKAY.
HEY, C'MON IN... YOU DON'T HAVE TO WAIT OUT THERE!
WOOF WURF
THAT'S OKAY...LET'S GO.
SORRY TO KEEP YOU WAITING!
.....
MAISON IKKOKU

.....
MAISON IKKOKU

HEH
SPARKLE

DON'T WORRY... I'LL BRING HER BACK BEFORE LONG.
HAVE A GOOD TIME, YOU TWO.

HNRGG!
VRMMMM
itamin

HEY, WASN'T THAT COACH MITAKA JUST NOW?
YOU BETCHA !

SAYYY... WHAT'S GOING ON WITH THOSE TWO?
WHAT DO YOU MEAN?
YOU KNOW... THE OTHER DAY AT THE TENNIS CLUB WHEN COACH MITAKA SAID...
MAISON IKKOKU
OH, THAT.
I WANT TO PAIR WITH YOU... FOR LIFE.
WELL! SOUNDS LIKE A PROPOSAL TO ME!
YOU THOUGHT SO TOO, HUH?
YEAH, THAT'S PRETTY MUCH WHAT I FIGURED, AS WELL.
WHAT DID KYOKO THINK?
SHE DIDN'T GET IT AT ALL.
OH, COME ON!
DON'T YOU THINK SHE'S JUST PLAYING DUMB?
MAISON IKKOKU
HMM... YEAH, MAYBE.
RIGHT! I HADN'T THOUGHT OF THAT!

IF SHE KNEW IT WAS A MARRIAGE PROPOSAL AND WAS JUST PLAYING DUMB...
...THEN I GUESS WE CAN ASSUME THAT THE ANSWER AT THIS POINT IN TIME IS "NO."
THERE'S STILL HOPE!
BRINGG
HELLO, MAISON IKKOKU...
TING
YUSAKU GODAI!! WHAT KIND OF AWFUL CHILD ASKS TO SPEAK WITH HIS MOTHER THEN JUST HANGS UP?!
LOOK, MOM, LEMME GET STRAIGHT TO THE POINT--
MONEY!!
I HAVEN'T GOTTEN MY CHECK THIS MONTH YET!
....
MOM? HELLO?
I FORGOT.
WHA?
MOM!!

WHAT A LOVING MOTHER!
WOWF!
IF IT WAS ME, I'D DUMP MY HUSBAND AND MARRY HIM IN A MINUTE! IN A SECOND!
BWA HA HA HA
GEEZ... THEY'RE STILL YAKKING!
I HEAR HE'S GOT A HUGE CONDO RIGHT DOWNTOWN...
NICE CAR, TOO.
....
I HEAR HIS FATHER IS SOME INDUSTRIAL TYCOON... THINK IT'S TRUE?
THAT'S WHAT THEY SAY, ALL RIGHT.
HE'S SO HANDSOME, AND SO NICE!
GRADUATED WITH HONORS FROM THE BEST UNIVERSITY!
I MEAN, YOU JUST COULDN'T FIND A MORE PERFECT MAN IF YOU TRIED!!
OH, I DIDN'T SEE YOU THERE.
HEAVENS, WHAT A FACE TO BE WEARING AT THIS TIME OF THE DAY!
YOU'RE YOUNG! PUT ON A SMILE!
YEAH, YOUR YOUTH IS ABOUT ALL YOU'VE GOT GOING FOR YOU!
AFTER WHAT THEY SAID ABOUT MITAKA...
...THEY COULDN'T POSSIBLY MAKE ME FEEL ANY WORSE!

Kosaku Matsuyama
Tadanari Tamogi
Otoko Kumino
Ryoko Kandagawa
Midori Setouchi
Hanako Shimokita
WELL, WE'RE SIGNED IN.
YEP... TIME TO HIT THE ROAD, EH?
NOODLES
MAN...ISN'T THERE MORE TO LIFE?
WHAT'S WRONG WITH IT?
SURE WISH I COULD GRADUATE RIGHT NOW...
ARE YOU KIDDING? BEING A STUDENT BEATS THE REAL WORLD.
YEAH, BUT YOU DON'T GET TREATED LIKE AN ADULT.
SO WHAT? YOU DON'T HAVE ANY RESPONSIBILITIES, EITHER.

AND YOU DON'T HAVE ANY REAL INCOME...
THAT'S TRUE, BUT AT LEAST YOU CAN BLOW WHAT YOU HAVE.
HEY...
WHAT?
HOW CAN YOU SIT THERE STUFFING YOUR FACE WITH DECENT FOOD WHILE ALL I CAN AFFORD IS THIS OLD DINNER ROLL?
I AIN'T SHARING A BITE, PAL.
"PAL," HE CALLS ME...
HEY, DIDN'T YOU WANT A TASTE OF THE REAL WORLD?
LEND ME A COUPLE OF BUCKS.
SHEESH, ALL YOU HAD TO DO WAS ASK.
I'VE BEEN THINKING OF BUYING A HOUSE.
KSSHH
REALLY!

BUT ISN'T YOUR CONDO EASIER TO TAKE CARE OF...?
WHILE I'M LIVING ALONE, YES...
ANYWAY, I'D LIKE A YARD, TOO.
SOUNDS GREAT.
AS **BIG** A YARD AS I CAN GET.
AND OFF IN A DISTANT CORNER OF THAT YARD...
...I'D KEEP A DOG.
REALLY?
YOU LIKE DOGS...
Y...YES. PARTICULARLY B-BIG DOGS...? LIKE MR. SOICHIRO.

Yap Yap Yap Yap Yap
HM... ?

OH !
FUZZY, COME BACK!
YAP YAP YAP
OH, YOU'RE SO CUTE !
HUF HUF HUF
SORRY TO BOTHER YOU!

SHUN, LOOK!
ISN'T HE CUTE?
HA HA, CUTE, YES, YOU BET, CUTE, THAT'S THE WORD!
BLOOSH
?

UMM...WASN'T THAT A BIT UNCOMFORTABLE?
AW, NO... I LOVE THE OCEAN!
YAP YAP
SPLUCH
KYOKO...

THE ONLY DOG I'D EVER KEEP IS MR. SOICHIRO.
UMM...

DO YOU SEE WHAT I'M GETTING AT, HERE?
WELL, KINDA...
KSSHH
I'M NOT ASKING YOU TO GIVE ME YOUR DOG, IF THAT'S WHAT YOU'RE THINKING.
OKAY?
IN A ROUNDABOUT WAY, I'M ASKING YOU TO MARRY ME.
SKSSHH
I THOUGHT SO!

I...I REALLY DON'T KNOW WHAT TO SAY.
I UNDERSTAND.
I CAN WAIT TWO OR THREE MORE YEARS.
I'M SORRY.
DON'T WORRY ABOUT IT.
I FIGURE IN TWO OR THREE MORE YEARS I CAN FINALLY CURE MYSELF OF MY FEAR OF DOGS.
KSSHH
OH, DON'T BE SHY, DEAR-- EAT AS MUCH AS YOU LIKE!
THANKS... I APPRECIATE IT.
NANAO
DOES MY HEART GOOD TO SEE A YOUNG MAN EATING THAT WAY!
EATING LIKE A PIG, YOU MEAN!
SHUT UP, YOSUKE, YOU BRAT!

ACTUALLY, THE ONLY REASON I'M EATING AT KOZUE'S HOUSE...
...IS PURE ACCIDENT!

I BUMPED INTO HER AT THE STATION AND...
WOW! YUSAKU! WHAT LUCK!
KOZUE. HEY.
COME ON OVER TO MY PLACE!
BUT...
MARK
MISUN
YOU CAN HAVE DINNER WITH US, OKAY?
FOOD...

I MEAN, IT'S NOT LIKE I ONLY CAME FOR THE FREE...OKAY, OKAY, SO I DID!
IT'S ALL BECAUSE I'M POOR.

SO, YUSAKU. WHAT'S YOUR MAJOR?
E-EDUCATION, SIR.
YEN

REALLY? DO YOU PLAN TO BECOME A TEACHER?
WELL, ER...I'M NOT SURE YET.
MAYBE A BUSINESSMAN?
WELL...
YEN
YOU KNOW, REGARDLESS OF WHAT I END UP DOING, I'D LIKE TO HAVE A REAL HAPPY HOME.
!
INSTEAD OF HITTING THE BAR AFTER WORK, I'D COME STRAIGHT HOME.
I'D LIKE TWO KIDS... A BOY AND A GIRL.
AND ON MY DAYS OFF, I'D WANT TO SPEND TIME WITH MY WIFE.
AND EVEN IF I HAVE TO COMMUTE FOR HOURS, I'D LIKE TO RENT A NICE HOUSE WITH A BIG YARD...
...AND KEEP A DOG.
HAPPY FAMILY:
SINGLE-FAMILY HOUSE w/DOG
BOWF!
MR. SOICHIRO
MY GOODNESS, YOU CERTAINLY HAVE A CLEAR VISION FOR YOUR FUTURE, DEAR!
I LIKE DOGS!

BETTER THAN BEING A WORKAHOLIC AND NEGLECTING YOUR FAMILY, I GUESS...
HMM... A "STAY-AT-HOME" HUSBAND, EH?
OH, BUT A WIFE IS *MUCH* HAPPIER THAT WAY, HONEY!
BLUP BLUP
WELL, THAT TYPE OF HUSBAND WOULD BE BETTER FOR KOZUE, ANYWAY.
HEY SIS, COULD YOU HANDLE BEING POOR?
AW, C'MON--I COULD MANAGE ON A BUDGET, SURE!
THAT'S TRUE...SHE'S SUCH A SENSITIVE GIRL.
....
WELL, YOU HAVE TO GRADUATE FIRST, DON'T YOU?
YEAH... I'VE GOT THREE MORE YEARS LEFT, HUH?
THREE LONG YEARS...
HONESTLY, MRS. ICHINOSE, YOU'RE SO *NOSY!*
HEY, I'VE GOT SERIOUS REASONS FOR ASKING, YOU KNOW!
Nezameyu
WE JUST TOOK A WALK ON THE BEACH AND TALKED ABOUT DOGS...AND THAT'S *ALL*.
SO HE DIDN'T PROPOSE TO YOU...
...IN A DIRECT WAY?
AH, HA... HE *DID*, DIDN'T HE?!
IT'S WRITTEN ON YOUR FACE.

KYOKO... ?
OH, HI! JUST COMING HOME?
EH?
THAT'S NOT THE ROAD FROM THE STATION... WHERE HAVE YOU BEEN?
NONE OF YOUR BEESWAX!
YOU'RE SUCH A **SNOOP**, AREN'T YOU?!

HAH! TRYING TO ESCAPE, HUH?
ET SHOP
COME ON, LET'S GO GO GO!
UH, SURE.

WHEW... THAT WOMAN!
WELL, DRINKING AND GOSSIPING SEEM TO BE HER REASONS FOR LIVING, DON'T THEY?

AS IF ANYONE CARES ABOUT **ME**.
WELL, ACTUALLY ***I*** DO...

ANYWAY, THERE'S NO POINT IN TRYING TO TALK ME INTO ANYTHING RIGHT NOW.
I DON'T KNOW HOW THINGS WILL CHANGE, AS TIME GOES BY...
...BUT FOR NOW...
AHH, THIS FEELS NICE.
HMM...
SKREE SKREE
"AS TIME GOES BY"...
SKREE

THREE MORE YEARS.
I...I WANT YOU TO STAY AS YOU ARE FOR JUST THREE MORE YEARS.
THREE YEARS...?
SOICHIRO WILL FLOW AWAY ALONG WITH THE TIME...
...AND THEN... AND THEN I...

JUST THREE YEARS ?!
YOU'VE GOTTA BE KIDDING !
WHATEVER DO YOU THINK WILL OCCUR IN A MERE THREE YEARS?

SURELY YOU DO NOT IMAGINE THAT ONCE YOU GRADUATE, A BRIGHT FUTURE WILL SIMPLY OPEN UP BEFORE YOU?
YEAH! BESIDES, YOU REALLY FIGURE YOU'RE ACTUALLY GONNA GRADUATE IN ONLY THREE YEARS?!
URK!

INDEED, YOU MAY NOT FIND A JOB UPON GRADUATION.
WILL IT REALLY BE POSSIBLE FOR YOU TO SUPPORT A FAMILY RIGHT OUT OF UNIVERSITY?
MAN, YOU SURE DON'T HAVE A CLEAR VISION OF YOUR FUTURE, DO YA?!
HNNK!
....
ER, KYOKO... COULD YOU WAIT FIVE MORE YEARS?
FIVE, OKAY ?
HMM ?
WUFF?
PEN-PAL
END